Volker Bach

The Landsknecht Cookbook

Zauberfeder Verlag, Braunschweig, Germany

Volker Bach
Landsknecht Cookbook
Original title "Landsknecht-Kochbuch"

1st Edition 2022

Text: Volker Bach
Food-Styling: Tino Kalning
Photos: Jens Christoph, except for those mentioned under Photo Credits
Translation: Volker Bach
Language editor: Scott Gissendanner
Editor: Stephan Naguschewski
Art director: Christian Schmal
Art editor: Heike Philipp, Christian Schmal
Production: Tara Tobias Moritzen
Printing: UAB BALTO print, Vilnius

Photo Credits
acrogame (Adobe Stock): Daniel Hopfer (16th century), page 3 • Marc Andryuk, page 5 • acrogame (Adobe Stock): Hans Sebastian Beham (1592), page 6–7 • acrogame (Adobe Stock): Daniel Hopfer (16th century), page 10 • Marion McNealy: Lucas Cranach der Ältere (1542), page 13, 15, 20, 32 • Marion McNealy: Erhard Schoen (1535), page 17 • Tatjana Junker, page 18 • Thomas Rebel, page 19, 21, 27, 30, 46, 114 • New Arfica (Adobe Stock), page 23 • Liam Quin (DeviantArt), page 158.

Printed in Lithuania
ISBN 978-3-96481-016-8
www.zauberfeder.com

Volker Bach

The Landsknecht Cookbook

Zauberfeder

Contents

LANDSKNECHT FOODWAYS

Landsknecht Foodways

Why this book?

People tend to have a clear idea of Landsknecht soldiers. Aggressive and fiercely masculine in their extravagantly slashed and puffed finery, they were a popular subject of contemporary art. Their image in popular music has helped spread a similar view. Look for them in any number of streaming services, and you will find rousing tunes of battle, of victory or death, male comradeship, and a heroic disdain for soft civilians. Unfortunately—or fortunately, if your interest is serious living history—the traditional view of the Landsknecht is largely detached from reality. The songs most influential in creating it were mostly written in the early twentieth century, under the impression of the First World War. When Albert Meinhardt published a collection of documented Landsknecht songs from sixteenth-century sources in 1979, they painted a very different picture. The joys and misfortunes of daily life were the most common focus in these tunes. They mention battle and loot, but also cold, hunger, gnawing poverty, and again and again, food and drink: cool wine, roast chickens, pork, eggs, bacon soup,

and the disparaged peasant fare that people joined the Landsknechts to avoid. As one popular ditty had it:

(In service) with the farmer, I must thresh and eat sour milk
With the king, I carry heavy bottles, with the farmer coarse clothing.

This may come as a surprise to some readers, but the sources clearly show that Landsknechts enjoyed good eating. 'A hard bed for good food' *(Hart ligen für gute Speiß)* is used to describe their life in the *Lied von der Kriegsleut Orden* (Meinhardt 9), and a Swiss song celebrating their victory at Dornach in 1499 mocks the Landsknecht enemy for paying more attention to cooking food than posting sentries. The military writer Leonhart Fronsperger (not to be confused with the general Georg von Frundsberg) advises commanders to pay particular attention to adequate supplies. Poorly fed Landsknechts were even more prone to mutiny than usual (Fronsperger CLVII v). This book will look at the Landsknecht soldiers and their world, especially at the food they hoped to earn through their hard and dangerous service.

Much ink has been spilled over the question of what exactly a Landsknecht was and was not. The fine details do not matter much for our purposes. The word was used at the time to describe German (not Swiss) foot soldiers who served for pay on a monthly basis, not as retainers to a lord or city government. Their pay was high, but Landsknecht service was not a stable job. Many returned to civilian employment when 'the war had a hole' and mercenaries were not required. Others spent these periods, especially in winter, begging or stealing. When the recruiters called once again for a muster, Landsknechts showed up more or less fully equipped to join the colours.

More than this, 'Landsknecht' was a group identification. Being a Landsknecht made you part of a world defined by its own rituals, traditions, and laws, not unlike that of sailors. This world was male-dominated (though far from exclusively male) and violent, but it was not anarchic. Landsknecht soldiers were judged in their own courts, and they elected comrades to represent their interests with the authorities. They were well known for being mutinous and not above downing tools ahead of crucial engagements in order to negotiate better pay. The adjective *landsknechtisch* described their attitude to life: their strong ego and touchy pride, the pleasure they took in showing off and taking risks, and a tendency towards excess in clothing, alcohol, and food. The last makes them as interesting a culinary subject as a sartorial one.

This book's focus on Landsknechts does not mean that it deals only with culinary habits exclusive to them. They were always part of a larger world, had families, homes, and civilian occupations whose habits they shared. By and large, the foodways of sixteenth-century Germany were also theirs, and in order to reconstruct what Landsknechts ate, we must also understand their social, cultural, and natural environment. It was one they shared with many others, from princely retainers whose generous food and clothing allowances reflected the status of their employers to a shifting population of vagrants who braved the dangers of the open road alongside them, and, of course, everyone else who was part of their armies: horsemen, gunners, sutlers, army wives, and the despised Schaufelbauern recruited to work as sappers. The conditions under which they lived together shaped the culinary habits of the soldiery.

The Landsknecht Army

Military writers of the sixteenth and seventeenth centuries have left us many detailed descriptions of the elaborate command structures governing Landsknecht armies. It is uncertain to what extent these reflect wishful thinking rather than reality. Yet, even allowing for a degree of exaggeration, it is clear that an army of such size needed a great deal of organisation. Technically, Landsknechts were independent contractors who provided their own arms and were individually responsible for their own supplies, but the fact that thousands or tens of thousands of them were assembled in one place made a systematic approach to supply management necessary.

Armed with pikes, halberds, arquebuses, and crossbows, the Landsknechts were always only part of an army composed of infantry, cavalry, and artillery. As a body, they served under an *Obrist* who had hired them and paid their wages. The *Obrist* in turn was under contract to the belligerent prince and received monthly payments for the maintenance of his forces. He was served by a staff of senior officers: the *Schultheiß* (the word literally means a magistrate) adjudicating dispute and administering justice, the *Profoss* (provost) who maintained order in camp, and the *Trosswaibel* or *Hurenwaibel* (sergeant of the train or sergeant of whores) in charge of the civilian supply train. Larger armies also had further officers such as *Quartiermeister* and *Proviantmeister* in charge of quartering and supplies. The Landsknecht force itself was divided into *Fähnlein*, units of several hundred men under a *Hauptmann*. All these officers received generous stipends and pay for a personal retinue that invariably included a personal cook.

Within their *Fähnlein*, the Landsknechts were organised in *Rotten*, units of six to ten men about whose workings we know regrettably little. They were formed and administered independently by the men who joined them and elected their leader, the *Rottmeister*. A *Rotte* was quartered together, sometimes shared sumpter horses or wagons for their baggage, and may even have managed its own food supply jointly. Our sources are largely silent on such arrangements, similar to messes among sailors and soldiers in later armies, but they surely would have made sense. We also know that in garrisons, some rations were issued to the *Rotte*, not the individual soldier.

The Landsknecht soldiers of each *Fähnlein* also elected a *Gemeinwaibel* to represent their interests vis-á-vis the *Hauptmann* and his right hand man, the *Feldwaibel* (a word that has survived to mean a sergeant in the German military today). Such a level of democratic participation and self-organisation in the military is rarely found in any other period of history.

A Landsknecht army never consisted of soldiers alone. To function, it required an extensive civilian supply train. Along with the baggage of officers and men, this included the *Schaufelbauern*—peasants recruited to dig earthworks and do other menial labour—soldiers' wives, and civilian camp followers of various kinds. Unlike a modern military force, a Landsknecht army had no centralised system of supplying food, equipment, and shelter, leaving individual soldiers entirely reliant on these services. Civilian merchants, smiths, tailors, shoemakers, food vendors, and cooks supplied them through the camp market. Under these circumstances, even an army that had enough wagons to manage the baggage of all officers and men—something that was far from the rule—could not hope to move fast. The economic flexibility that a military force based on short-term contracts offered its employers was paid for in cumbersome arrangements, waste of resources, and limited strategic options.

The one group that no Landsknecht army could have functioned without were its many women camp followers. Contemporary sources often refer to them simply as *Huren*, and the fact that this word means 'whore' in modern German illustrates how the meanings and associations of words can shift over time. Though

some observers may have assumed so, it is certain that not all, and not even most *Huren* were prostitutes. Many lived in temporary, unofficial marriages with soldiers that were recognised in military regulations. Others made a living selling beer or brandy, or by washing and mending clothes. The camp market also provided demand for prostitution, but it was far from the only employment option for women. Especially indispensable to the army was the labour of soldiers' wives. An eyewitness account from the Turkish wars describes them carrying spare clothing and shoes, canvas shelter pieces, pans, pots, bowls, and firewood gathered up along the way on their backs. In camps or quarters, they were busy washing, cooking, and mending, and they certainly also participated in the petty larceny and looting that armies of the time were infamous for.

THE CAMP MARKET

The Camp Market

The traditional pay of a Landsknecht was four Rhenish guilders a month for *'Sold, Kost und Schaden'*, as the Diet of Constance decreed in 1507. This meant he was obliged to provide his own food, clothing, and equipment from this. Employers passed on these responsibilities to their troops in return for relatively generous pay and expected them to meet their needs through the civilian market. This was impossible in practice. The resources of a largely agricultural society did not stretch to easily accommodating thousands of extra mouths even in good years, and the infrastructure to transport food was often patchy. Unless seaports or navigable rivers allowed for transport by ship, goods had to be carried slowly and expensively over often poor roads. Lazarus von Schwendi, an experienced commander, writes that 1,000 wagons had to enter camp every ten days just to provide the bread for a large army (Frauenholz 266). These dimensions are difficult to envision almost anywhere, and leaving such logistics to the free market would have ensured failure in short order. The larger the army, the greater the need for careful organisation and planning.

Thus, though Landsknechts did not receive rations, their commanders still had to ensure they had enough to eat. Contemporary sources give us an idea of the quantities required. Military writers estimate a daily consumption of 1–2 lbs of bread, 1–1 ½ lbs of meat and a generous quantity of beer. Some also add weekly amounts of bacon, cheese, butter, and salt that are equally ample, but not unrealistic. Ensuring that these foodstuffs reliably reached army camps, especially while the troops were on the move, was a considerable challenge even for the commanders of small forces. The scale matched that of provisioning a medium-sized or major city, though it had to be achieved without recourse to the infrastructure that had grown up organically to supply towns.

To solve this problem, the army's *Proviantmeister* and *Profoss* had to work together closely. The *Proviantmeister* corresponded with merchants, city councils, and territorial princes to negotiate free market access, toll-free travel for his suppliers, and deliveries of needed supplies in bulk. As much as possible, he tried to announce the presence of an army in advance in order to give merchants and artisans time to prepare. Traders received safe conduct papers and sometimes even cavalry escorts to ensure their safe arrival. Such negotiations were always carried out with the unspoken threat that absent deliveries, soldiers could simply take whatever they needed by force, but plunder on such a scale was not a sustainable business model. Infamous though Landsknechts might be for looting and extortion, they were also good customers to the peasants, craftsmen, and merchants supplying their camps.

The *Profoss* and his club-wielding *Steckenknechte* policed the camp market. It was the responsibility of the *Profoss* to set maximum prices, an exercise that required striking the difficult balance between the needs of the men and the willingness of traders to continue supplying them. He also collected market dues, assigned stalls, ensured quality standards, and enforced the use of honest measures. Cavalrymen under his command patrolled the roads to the camp to secure access and prevent merchants from buying up supplies in order to corner the market. In principle, a camp market was regulated much as it would have been in a contemporary city. We do not know how far it was ever possible to realise this, but considering the sudden spike in demand an army produced, the requirement to work with unfamiliar measures, and the fact that customers were armed and accustomed to violence, it surely cannot have been easy.

Although setting prices was daily practice, we know very little about the goods sold in camp markets or the prices at which they retailed. We thus have no way of telling how profitable this business would have been compared to a regular urban market. The historian Hans-Michael Möller used the only surviving set of prices charged during the siege of Metz in 1552 to calculate that the greater part of a Landskecht's pay would have been spent on food alone (Möller 161 ff). We must bear in mind, however, that prices varied greatly and the only data we have come from a prolonged siege and may well be unrepresentative.

Surely, we must imagine a camp market sparsely furnished, improvised, and chaotic in spite of all efforts to impose order. Contemporary pictures rarely show purpose-built market stalls. Instead, merchants walk around or sell goods from their wagons and carts. Cooking fires and improvised tents are distributed haphazardly, and most equipment appears very basic. None of this comes as a surprise when we consider how difficult transporting goods and gear was. Most likely such a place had little in common with an orderly urban market of the time, and even less with a modern marketplace.

Des Landgraff
dte: fier hauptma

Sutlers, Pedlars, and Camp Followers

Lacking permanent buildings and resident artisans, a camp market likely looked more like a village market or temporary fair. It was also served differently. Bread was sourced from bakers from the surrounding area and carried to the market on foot for sale whenever possible. The sheer scale of that endeavour must have presented a challenge even where village ovens and town bakeries had excess capacity and grain was plentiful. Meat, on the other hand, could hardly be transported over long distances without refrigeration. Instead, live animals were brought to the camp to be slaughtered and processed. This was the business of the *Sudler*, from whose name we get the word 'sutler'.

Sudler or *Garköche* (the former term derives from the word *Sud* for a cooking broth) were also an established part of urban markets. There, they either bought meat from guilded butchers or, where this was permitted, did their own slaughtering, cooked it, and sold it in individual portions. This activity was usually heavily regulated and supervised by the butchers' guilds who jealously guarded their own privileges, something that must have made the freer air of a Landsknecht camp attractive to such cooks. Sources on the day-to-day reality of their business are sparse. Illustrations and surviving price regulations both suggest that they sold meat together with some accompanying vegetables and legumes cooked in the broth. Their culinary qualifications are equally uncertain. Cooks' guilds were often associated with or subordinate to those of butchers, so they very likely had some way of acquiring the relevant skills to process meat. The detailed ordinance regulating the guild of house butchers and cooks for the city of Hamburg, however, makes no mention of a formal apprenticeship. We do not know how members gained their qualification. The importance of skilled butcher-cooks for supplying armies was recognised by contemporaries, however. When the towns of Thuringia joined the rebellion during the Peasant War of 1525, cooks were one thing they provided to the rebel army. The Hamburg ordinance, too, required guild members to serve the city council on campaign and at sea.

To get into business, a *Sudler* needed capital. Cauldrons, pans, pots, and spits were required, they had to be transported, cattle had to be bought and herded, ingredients and fuel provided. Once all that was in place, their actual work was quite similar to what happened in urban cookshops or what hired butchers did for their clients. Bones were boiled for broth, stomachs and guts used for sausages and puddings, offal turned into various dishes, and the most expensive muscle meat either boiled or roasted. The *New Kochbuch* by Marx Rumpolt published in 1581 proudly gives long lists of recipes detailing what to do with every part of a given animal. Though a camp cook likely had fewer skills and possibilities than the personal cook of an elector-archbishop, the same principle applied. Getting the most out of an animal was in the *Sudler's* economic interest, at least unless successful looting briefly flooded the market with cheap cattle.

We know even less about the personal cooks belonging to officers' retinues. They enjoyed generous pay—up to twice a common Landskecht's—and conspicuous status. These men were very likely recruited from among the artisanal butcher-cooks that also provided the *Sudler*, though their task was very different. They served a small but demanding clientele and likely had access to more varied equipment. Every senior officer was allowed a wagon to carry his personal baggage, so bringing along specialised tools would not have presented great difficulty. Members of the upper class frequently travelled with cooks in civilian life as well, so the skill set required to feed them in proper style was part of their professional training.

The opposite end of the social spectrum was inhabited by the petty regraters of food and drink, often women who bought them in larger quantities and resold them in individual portions. This was a familiar part of the ecosystem of urban poverty, where poor women sold desalinated herrings and individual slices of bacon to the even more desperate. Absent the control of guilds and town ordinances limiting options, the sale of alcoholic beverages could be lucrative in camp markets. Some foods such as fritters and waffles, too, could be prepared with limited equipment and sold at a profit. Neither was a road to riches, though.

The camp market also supplied all those who did their own cooking. This applied not least to many of the soldiers' wives who carried their own cooking equipment and needed somewhere to buy ingredients. *Sudler* and butchers slaughtered animals in the camp and sold their meat, peasants from nearby villages brought their produce, and pedlars offered sugar, spices, and brandy among a host of other articles. If the Landsknechts really cooked and ate together in their *Rotte*, they could shop here much like householders did in town markets.

The Field Kitchen

Written sources tell us little about how people cooked in Landsknecht camps. Since no military administration was in charge of providing rations, there are no surviving kitchen accounts. As with clothing, we get much of our information from pictures, and in both cases it is far from certain that what they show is in any way representative. What we do find is that kitchen equipment and cooking scenes feature with great regularity whenever camps and supply trains are shown. The way that blazing cookfires and bubbling cauldrons are invariably part of their camps reinforces the stereotype of the Landsknechts as voracious and demanding eaters.

We should generally imagine field cooking arrangements as very basic. Transport capacity required to carry equipment was expensive. Fronsperger records the monthly expense for a single baggage wagon at 24 guilders, six months' pay for a common foot soldier (Fronsperger XXXVIII r). Thus, it is likely even *Sudler* would have limited themselves to what was strictly necessary. The illustrations generally agree. We see cauldrons, pots, and pans used over open fires, but hardly ever any tables or benches. This is not inherently unrealistic; experienced cooks do not need much equipment to produce a large variety of dishes. The women we often see depicted cooking with small pots and pans, very likely soldiers' wives, also would have had experience with such limited facilities. Estate lists show that poor households often owned little more than a pot, a pan, and a few bowls—roughly the utensils mentioned in descriptions and often shown in woodcuts. Most Landsknechts came from a milieu of relative poverty, so their female companions would have known how to make do with this.

To learn more about this cooking gear, we must once again turn to images. What we see is not appreciably different than what contemporary pictures of domestic and professional kitchens show. The famous illustrations of an army supply train in Altdorfer's woodcut series *Triumphzug Kaiser Maximilians* shows enormous cauldrons carried on wagons while heavily burdened camp followers carry smaller pots in baskets on their backs. Other pictures of soldiers' wives show them carrying pots, pans, and spits while wooden spoons protrude from their packs. Camp scenes show cooking done over open fires, often depicted as blazing with bright flame and thick smoke. Cauldrons are suspended from wooden racks directly or on ratchet hooks. Flat-bottomed pottery cookpots suitable for slowly stewing soups, legumes, and porridges stand by the fires. Spits and pans are held in readiness or used. Mortars and the three-legged cast metal *Grapen* we frequently find mentioned in contemporary inventories and cookbooks are rarely seen. This is not surprising given their weight, and it suggests that these illustrations are at least partly based on actual observation.

Large cauldrons and pots by roaring fires very likely depict the kitchens of *Sudler* cooks feeding hundreds. Smaller cookfires showing multiple pots or pans raise the question whether they are meant to produce food for sale, or whether a *Rotte* of Landsknechts is preparing a shared meal here. Either is plausible. We know that artillerymen had the privilege of cooking by their guns, something that would have been impractical to do with hundreds of small individual fires. Finally, there are depictions of women working with single pots or pans over small fires. These are likely soldiers' wives cooking for a single Landsknecht or a small group. What we never see are Landsknechts themselves using these arrangements. Men are only ever shown cooking in large vessels which probably makes them *Sudler*. This need not mean that Landsknechts could not cook. In a remark on the subject of bread, Hieronymus Bock points out that you could learn from experienced soldiers how to bake bread on hot stones. Resourcefulness in the face of shortage was surely something Landsknecht service taught.

Officers' cooks seldom had such worries, if at all. They served the culinary needs of an employer who had access to an entire baggage wagon and did not need to handle the large quantities a *Sudler* did. This would have allowed them to serve the more refined cuisine of their day. Their masters were among the few in the army who had regular access to tables, seating, and serving dishes and to complex cooking equipment such as baking pans designed to be heated with embers from above and below like a modern Dutch oven, mortars, sieves, mixing bowls, roasting spits, and chopping knives. The technical possibilities of a well-stocked camp kitchen are illustrated in the pictures that accompany the cookbook *Opera* by Bartolomeo Scappi published in 1570. Landsknecht officers probably did not travel in the same style as popes, but their arrangements were hardly primitive.

We also need to remember that Landsknecht soldiers did not only cook in camp. Troops were quartered in civilian households when in enemy country, and sometimes also in nominally friendly areas. Here, they would be able to use the kitchens of their involuntary hosts and help themselves to their supplies, no doubt doing considerable damage. Storing up food was common practice in affluent homes in both town and country, and a group of soldiers who did not expect to stay long were able to go through a year's supply of sausages, meat, fruit, cheese, butter, wine, brandy, and firewood in short order.

The question of fuel, which in practice meant firewood, was another logistical headache. Timber in sixteenth-century Germany was a scarce resource that was jealously guarded and sold dearly. The blazing fires we see in many illustrations must have struck observers as wasteful. We do not know where the Landsknechts got their firewood. An observer notes that women camp followers picked up pieces along the march, but this method can hardly have sufficed to supply a large army moving slowly. There surely was looting, and locals must have been persuaded to sell their supply not least by the prospect of otherwise losing it without compensation. We know that soldiers in later centuries sometimes tore down entire buildings to burn the timber. Lack of firewood must have become an acute problem especially for large armies staying in one place. Alternative fuels hardly featured. Although Fronsperger writes that charcoal is preferable to wood because it does not produce smoke that can betray an army's position to the enemy (Fronsperger CLIX v), its high price and limited availability made it impractical on a large scale. Officers' cooks may have used it, and no doubt blacksmiths and other artisans in the camp market did, but it could not have served as a general cooking fuel.

One final remark on the question of bread supply is called for. Fronsperger describes mobile ovens made of copper that could accompany an army in the field (Fronsperger XCII r). This was technically possible, but the sheer scale of the demand makes it unlikely that they were ever widespread enough to make a difference. We know that armies sometimes seized ovens in the vicinity of their camp to bake bread when supplies fell short. Improvised solutions such as baking flatbreads on hot stones or under upturned bowls must also have been familiar. In the end, though, bread shortage frequently would have meant going without when deliveries from city bakers failed to arrive. Porridge could provide the required calories, but it was not felt to be an adequate substitute.

The German Larder

In 1550, the famous physician and botanist Hieronymus Bock published a book called *Teutsche Speißkammer* (The German Larder) in which he condemned fashionable Italian food and praised German cuisine as healthy and well-suited to all human needs. The book is interesting today above all because of the detailed descriptions and medical evaluations of common foods. In reading it, we need to remember that Bock was a wealthy man who lived in the Rhine valley, an area blessed with a mild and sunny climate. A greater variety of food plants could be grown here than anywhere else in Germany, and yet even here, peasants, labourers, and Landsknechts without access to the carefully tended market gardens catering to the rich had to make do with a limited selection. Season, geography, and the military situation dictated what reached them in camps or quarters, and supplies varied greatly. Nonetheless, Bock provides a useful overview of what foods were available at all.

BREAD

The daily bread of the Landsknecht differed little from that of the labourer or farmhand. It needed to be durable to be carried over long distances, and we know from household books that common bread was often baked in bulk and stored for weeks or months. It was made from the dominant bread grain of its region—rye in Northern Germany, wheat or spelt in the South. The flour was bolted to remove impurities and make it last longer, but it was far from the fineness achieved in modern flours. Salt, water, and sourdough were usually the only other ingredients. As we will see in the recipe section, the resulting bread not only served as a food in its own right, but also as an ingredient, e.g., in porridges and puddings and for thickening sauces.

Finer, lighter breads were surely available in or near towns where professional bakers were able to profitably specialise. Light wheat bread rolls known as *Wecken* or *Semmeln*, fine rye loaves, but also crisp pretzels and *Kringel* rings or breads enriched with milk or cheese were eaten on special occasions. *Lebkuchen*, a heavily spiced honey biscuit that was also used to thicken sauces at the time, is even expressly mentioned in a Landsknecht song (Meinhardt 34).

MEAT

The ability to eat meat was a matter of status in sixteenth-century Germany and therefore important to Landsknechts. Organising regular supplies took some logistical effort, but no excessive amount of labour, as animals could be brought to the market on the hoof. Long-distance cattle drives were familiar from civilian life as herds of oxen from Denmark and Hungary were delivered to German cities every year. While they campaigned in enemy country, Landsknechts would often loot livestock, the most valuable possession of many farmers. During the Peasant War of 1525, the glut of captured cattle drove down prices to the point that a cow sold for ⅓ of a guilder. However, a steady supply of affordable meat needed to be ensured even without access to plentiful plunder.

Along with the high-status lamb and venison, which most Landsknechts probably never tasted, the most coveted meats were beef and pork. Mutton and especially goat were eaten, but not esteemed highly. Poultry, on the other hand, was popular and accordingly expensive. Surviving price regulations show that the most expensive parts were sheer, roastable meat known as *Brät*. Meat that contained many bones or otherwise suitable only for stewing and offal were much more affordable. The situation in camp markets was surely similar. Since fresh meat did not last, it was sold and prepared immediately after slaughter. Laying in stores in this context meant for a *Sudler* maintaining a herd that accompanied the army on the march.

FISH

Unlike meat, fresh fish was felt to be a dispensable luxury. High-status fish especially—pike, trout, carp, salmon, and sturgeon—were limited to the tables of the wealthy. The only fish expressly mentioned in our sources as being eaten by Landsknechts are stockfish and the salted and dried soles known as *Plätteisen*, both imported from Scandinavia. These were not popular, and Fronsperger expressly states that it is better to lay in stores of any other food by preference because they spoiled easily, tasted vile, and had to be prepared with large quantities of expensive cooking fat (Fronsperger CLXII r). If they were served nonetheless, it was to observe church-mandated fast days. The same is likely true for salt herring imported from the North Sea. We do not know how seriously Landsknechts took the obligation to fast. Officially, the Catholic church prohibited meat and dairy products on Fridays and in the weeks of Lent and Advent. Especially pious Catholics also abstained on Wednesdays and Saturdays. The reformers led by Martin Luther, on the other hand, rejected all mandatory fasts, and the authorities in many parts of the country ceased to police compliance. In the 1590s, the court budget of Hessen-Kassel provided its soldiers both meat and fish on Wednesdays and Fridays, leaving the choice to the individual. Only Saturday was meat-free.

EGGS AND DAIRY

Fronsperger writes that soldiers who were served a meal of eggs, cheese, or bacon on a given day did not require any other meat (Fronsperger CLIX v). We must hope for his sake that his troops agreed. Eggs and dairy products, from the low-status clabbered *Sauermilch* associated with peasant fare to the expensive, imported parmesan cheese, played an important role in everyone's diet.

Cheese was produced in rural households and brought to town markets fresh for sale and immediate consumption. Camp markets would have attracted the same suppliers whose product resembled curds or cottage cheese. Hard mature cheese was also available, and some types were even traded over long distances. Parmesan from Italy was esteemed most highly, but Dutch and Swiss cheeses also sold in German markets. We know relatively little about these cheeses except that mild, fat varieties were highly appreciated. Cheese of this kind could be eaten with bread, but also used in soups, pastries, and fritters.

Butter was another important element of German cuisine. Hieronymus Bock remarked that it was needed where olives for oil did not grow (Bock LX r). Middle-class tables often featured a block of butter which diners were free to spread on bread or add to their foods. It also featured as an important ingredient in porridges and other cereal-based dishes. Butter was not usually sold fresh, but preserved for storage either by salting or clarifying. Fresh butter, known as May butter in many recipes, was regarded especially highly, however.

VEGETABLES

There was no category for vegetables in the culinary language of the Landsknecht world. The word *Gemüs* that describes them today referred to side dishes in general, including pasta, porridge, fritters, and cooked fruit. Numerous recipes collected under this term in cookbooks such as that by Marx Rumpolt show the variety that was subsumed here. Despite the semantic closeness to the word *Mus* meaning a soft, spoonable food, not everything was cooked to a mush.

Vegetables, part of the *Gemüs* category, were widely eaten and experiencing a considerable boost in status in the sixteenth century. Imported varieties and techniques brought things such as white asparagus or cauliflower to Germany, where they became status symbols. However, the selection offered by traditional cultivated and foraged plants could already be considerable, depending on the season. Hieronymus Bock provides the following list of vegetables and their availability:

SPRING

Spinach, chard, cabbage shoots, leaf lettuce, poppy leaves, orach, beet greens, bugloss, borage, parsley, *Körstel* (identity uncertain), dill, shallots, leeks, green onions, garlic, sorrel, lettuce, bistort, ribwort plantain, hogweed, cabbage thistle, marsh marigolds, violets, nettles, sow thistle, hops, asparagus, and rampion bellflower

SUMMER

Spinach, chard, orach, cabbage shoots, green leeks, fresh garlic, fresh onions, parsley roots, carrots, parsnips, skirrets, young beets, radishes, peascods, green beans, unripe grain, strawberries, blueberries, raspberries, sweet and sour cherries, early grapes and apples, early pears, summer-ripening plums, peaches, and mushrooms

AUTUMN

Cabbage, beets, melons, cucumbers, *Pfedem* (probably a type of melon), bottle gourd, Indian apples (probably New World squashes), green beans, black-eyed peas, peas, mulberries, plums, pears, sweet cherries, hazelnuts, walnuts, almonds, chestnuts, apples, quinces, peaches, medlars, service tree berries, sloes, and grapes

WINTER

Along with a host of preserved foods, watercress and cabbage are seasonal.

This list is not complete, and it does not apply to all of Germany. On the one hand, it lacks common garden herbs such as sage and marjoram that feature in many contemporary recipes. On the other hand, fruit such as mulberries, peaches, and almonds only grew in the climatically favoured regions of the upper Rhine valley. The mention of 'Indian apples', too, indicates that money and effort went into following horticultural fashion here. Common Landsknechts were not likely to sample these innovations. They depended on what the camp market provided, and on most days this would have been what was grown in quantity everywhere: *Kraut* and *Rüben*.

Kraut referred to all kinds of leafy greens, but above all the cabbage found in every kitchen. *Rüben* meant all kinds of root vegetables, mainly the various relatives of the turnip, grown in gardens throughout the land, but also carrots, parsley roots, skirrets, and other species. Assigning a specific type to the word is rarely possible. Both cabbage and turnips were cooked fresh or preserved by salt fermentation. The resulting sauerkraut was mainly a winter food, however, so it would not have featured prominently on the menu of Landsknechts during campaigning season.

Legumes also counted as *Gemüs*. The most common kinds were fava beans and peas which were normally dried for storage and softened by cooking, and it is likely that this is how they were sold in camp markets. Fresh green peas and fava bean pods—today's 'French' green beans are a New World crop—were a strictly seasonal pleasure.

Fruit came to market fresh and in large quantities. Since they were difficult to preserve, growers had to sell them quickly during the relatively short harvest season. Accordingly, they were only available for brief periods of time during the year. However, in the absence of large-scale market-gardening as became common in later centuries, it is unlikely there would have been enough to feed an entire army camp. As in the cities, fresh fruit brought to market in season probably represented a modest luxury within reach of many, but not everyone.

Contemporary writers also included cereal products like porridge and pasta in the category of *Gemüs*. These were common, though we should assume that more complex preparations like noodles or dumplings were high-end products and common Landsknecht soldiers more likely ate porridges. Some such recipes were practical even with limited equipment, however, as we will see in the case of *Zotten Mus* (see p. 51).

SEASONINGS

'Seasonings' first conjures up the image of expensive imported spices, but even simple foods were seasoned whenever possible, and likely skilfully. The first thing that needs mentioning in this context is salt. Salt served as a preservative as much as a seasoning and is listed among rations and supplies laid in for garrisons. Since soldiers in army camps neither fed large herds of cattle nor preserved meat, the quantity they needed for cooking could likely be made available without overtaxing the supply system. The second proverbial seasoning of the poor was vinegar. The term *Essig* was used in a broader sense than today. It could include vinegar and alegar, but also the juice of sloes or crabapples. Any sour condiment qualified.

Onions and garlic were further options for inexpensively spicing up food. Smelling of either was considered boorish, but this hardly stopped most people from indulging. Those who did not grow them in their own gardens—as practically all country people did—could buy onions in the market. This very likely also was true in army camps, though again the sudden concentration of demand must have overtaxed local supplies quite frequently.

Locally grown herbs were also popular in the kitchen. Many surviving recipes mention them, and Hieronymus Bock again gives us a list of what he considers indispensable in any kitchen garden: marjoram, wild thyme, garden thyme, rosemary, basil, oregano, hyssop, sage, mugwort, parsley, dill, chervil, and the unidentified *Frauenwurz*. Herbs were usually grown or foraged for private use, so it is unlikely there would have been enough to feed an army camp in any one place. They were also dried for preservation in households. People who did not manage their own supply would have found it difficult to just buy them, however. This fact may go some way towards explaining the attraction of commercially cooked food as well. Professional cooks would obviously keep a store of seasonings and ideally have the capital to invest in additions to the meal. Individual Landsknechts or their wives may well not have been able to.

Though prices were already declining, imported spices were still the most luxurious of seasonings. When they feature prominently in surviving recipes, it is a measure of how many recipe books addressed a wealthy clientele. Nonetheless, the highly spiced *Lebkuchen* (a variety of gingerbread) is mentioned in a Landsknecht song, and we know that pedlars sold spices in village markets. We should not exclude the possibility that spices found their way to camp markets and that *Sudler* cooks used them. Officers' cooks certainly did. Fronsperger also mentions stores of cloves, ginger, cinnamon, nutmeg, and saffron held for garrison troops, but expressly only for the use of the sick (Fronsperger CLIX v). In the everyday life of common soldiers, they were a luxury that was consciously, and most likely rarely, enjoyed. The same is true for honey and sugar, the most common sweeteners. When Hieronymus Bock complains that people have taken to using sugar excessively (Bock XXXII r), this surely refers to the kitchens of the wealthy only.

LORDS' FARE, PEASANTS' FARE

Lords' Fare, Peasants' Fare

What you eat depends not only on what you like or can afford. It also depends on what you consider appropriate for yourself. Something that looks like a proper meal from one perspective may seem an unconscionable luxury or barely better than animal feed from another. Sixteenth-century Germany made a clear mental distinction above all

between the food of the ruling class—*Herrenspeis*—and that of the peasantry—*Bauernspeis*. The upper class was able to indulge in a conspicuous luxury that no one else could hope to imitate. Their feasts included venison (limited by jealously guarded hunting rights), high-quality fish, sugar, spices, exotic vegetables, fresh fruit, and complex preparations. Lesser luxuries such as white bread, rice, fresh fish, and roast meat were daily fare to them. Some Landsknecht officers came from this background, and their generous pay would have allowed them to live in this style at least part of the time while they were employed. To the majority of common soldiers, these things were rare luxuries.

Yet social distinctions in food continued well below this divide. Though few of the modestly well-off could ever hope to serve true lordly fare, they distanced themselves from the truly poor by what they ate. Master artisans or landowning farmers ate differently from labourers and cottagers, and any town dweller, no matter how poor, would have rejected the suggestion that he ate peasant food. Bread and animal products played the most important role in this distinction. Leavened, oven-baked bread was the daily fare of townspeople and village landowners, The rural poor, or so prejudice had it, subsisted on porridge. The consumption of meat, eggs, and dairy products also tracked the social divide. Though the rural poor often kept chickens and goats, they had to sell the eggs and cheese they produced rather than eat them themselves. Peasants offering baskets of eggs or fresh goat cheeses were a familiar sight on town markets, and the rule that exempted vendors who carried their entire stock on their bodies from camp market dues was intended to attract them to the army's markets. Fresh meat, too, was a sign of distinction. It was rare in the rural economy, limited to the few slaughter days unless someone roasted a chicken to celebrate some occasion. Wealthy farmers laid in large stores of salted and smoked meat and sausages, something that must have been very attractive to looting soldiers. Smoking, the mark of the householder, was also appreciated purely for the flavour it imparted: We know that bratwurst sausages and the brined meat given to garrison troops were sometimes briefly smoked before cooking. This did nothing to preserve the food, but added flavour. Town markets concentrated demand to the point that animals were slaughtered every day. Anyone with the requisite money could have fresh meat daily, and though this was far from everyone, the number of people who could was not insignificant. On the other hand, only wealthy burghers had livestock to slaughter for themselves. In the context where most did not have this kind of wealth, smoked ham, not fresh beef, was the marker of greater prosperity.

Landsknechts occupied a privileged position in this continuum. We can trace the tradition that soldiers were entitled to bread and meat daily to at least the fifteenth century. To many others, this was at best a fond dream reflected in the words of fairy tales that promised daily roast and boiled meat to faithful servants. However poor a Landsknecht otherwise might be, he did not eat like a poor man.

Drink

While reconstructing the food habits of Landsknecht soldiers presents some difficulties, their drinking preferences are thoroughly attested in contemporary sources: they imbibed readily and in large quantities. Landsknechts enjoyed an unrivalled reputation as drunkards in a society where heavy alcohol consumption was normal for everyone. Surely, there must have been a basis in reality. Individual Landsknechts are attested with bynames such as 'always-full' or 'seek-drink,' and a proverb states that Landsknechts and pigs had to be 'full up' day and night. The question thus is not whether they drank, but what.

The most common beverage—at least outside the wine-growing regions of southwestern Germany—was beer. In sixteenth-century Germany, home brewing for household use or sale to neighbours was still common practice in rural areas. This kind of beer had little keeping quality and was generally not highly esteemed, but the sheer concentration of demand probably drew suppliers to camp markets. Buyers who had a choice, though, preferred commercially brewed beers. These brews mostly came from cities where local government enforced strict quality standards. It was on this kind of widely appreciated drink that the lawyer and connoisseur Heinrich Knaust wrote his *Fünnf Bücher von der [...] Kunst Bier zu Brauen* (Five Books on the Art of Brewing Beer) in 1575. Commercial beers were traded over long distances and sold at a commensurate markup. The most successful brew from the city of Einbeck was a distinct luxury product. It was transported 500 km overland to Munich, and the council of Hamburg profitably declared its sale a government monopoly. Other local brewing centres such as Hamburg or Braunschweig also enjoyed reputations that boosted sales beyond their region. However, the largest share of commercially brewed beer was intended for sale in the cities where they were brewed and their hinterlands. People generally distinguished between three types. The very strong, durable beers intended for export that Knaust calls 'proper' beer, the weaker and less long-lasting *Tafelbier* (table beer) that was mostly sold locally for immediate consumption, and the weak *Dünnbier* or *Kofent* that contained hardly any alcohol at all. Tafelbier, usually supplied to local hostelries, would have been well suited for sale in camp markets.

Along with beer, wine was a popular everyday beverage wherever it was grown in quantity. The supply, and thus the price, was more vulnerable to the vagaries of weather than it was for beer, but in average years, even servants and journeymen drank wine daily in the cities of the Rhine valley. As with beer, there were considerable differences in quality and cost. Fashionable Mediterranean imports such as *Malvasier* (Malmsey) or *Reinfal* (Ribolla gialla) were limited to the rich. Most people drank local production, mostly of recent vintage since these wines rarely kept

well. A Landsknecht army encamped in a wine-growing region would have been able to draw on copious local supplies that could be delivered through established infrastructure. Many illustrations of army camps show purpose-built cars loaded with large casks from which vendors drew drink directly into pitchers and cups. The 'cool wine' celebrated in Landsknecht songs was a distinctly realistic aspiration.

A newly fashionable drink of the age was *Branntwein*, distilled liquor. Landsknechts were so fond of it that Lazarus von Schwendi, a military writer of the late sixteenth century, vainly demanded its sale be banned in army camps (Frauenholz 31). One large advantage this brandy had over other beverages was that it could be produced even from sour beer, a brewer's failed wort, or the pomace left from wine pressing. As early as 1500, exports from the Rhineland were considerable. Though distilled liquor had already been known for centuries in principle, it had only become a widely available beverage quite recently, and as with all new drugs, a degree of moral panic ensued. In response, some city governments regulated sales quantities or banned drinking it in public, but neither rule was enforced in Landsknecht armies as far as we know. Poor women generated income by reselling it in small portions, a business that often shaded into prostitution. Sixteenth-century *Branntwein*, incidentally, had little to do with the cask-aged product known under that name today. It was sold fresh and more likely resembled a raw grappa or grain vodka.

Finally, we should not underestimate the importance of water as an everyday drink. Though it was considered improperly miserly for householders to let even servants drink water, doing so cannot have been uncommon among the poor. An army camp, though, was not a good environment for that. Crowded, but lacking the infrastructure of public wells or conduits that cities had, finding clean water must have been challenging. Unregulated rivers tended to be muddy at the best of times, and the dense traffic of people and horses around the camp stirred up extra dirt. Like in some cities, clean washing and drinking water may have been sold in markets, but more likely people made do without as best they could. When there was usable water, though, Landsknechts were as likely to drink it as anyone.

Of Tableless Table Manners

Table manners are not the first thing that comes to mind when we envision a Landsknecht eating, and this particular cliché is probably accurate. The age of Luther, as it is known in Germany, has acquired a deeply questionable reputation for poor conduct. The great reformer himself is popularly—and wrongly—quoted today as having said, 'Why are you not belching and farting, did you not enjoy the meal?'. In reality, a multitude of printed books and broadsheets on the subject suggests that interest in the subject was lively at the time. The rules as such did not differ substantially from those enshrined in late medieval texts. Diners were to wash their hands before sitting down to eat. They were not to annoy their companions by taking up undue space on often tightly packed benches, refrain from taking more than their share of particularly tempting dishes, and not do anything felt to be disgusting. People ate with knives, spoons, and their fingers, a practice that need neither be unappealing nor unhygienic. The medieval custom of sharing cups and plates was increasingly falling into abeyance. A meal at which these rules were followed competently would strike us as unusual, but not off-putting, let alone comically entertaining.

It is very unlikely that Landsknechts followed these rules, though. Nobody had the authority and power to force them, and they had nothing to gain by doing so. Interest in table manners was strongest among the urban burgher class who needed to distinguish themselves from the great unwashed. By contrast, foreign visitors wrote shocked reports of the table manners the German nobility displayed. Noblemen drank themselves into a stupor, smashed tableware, and spat cherry pits at each other—because they could. Who would stop them? This, of course, is exactly the attitude that *landsknechtisch* exemplifies. These were proud and recalcitrant men fond of display and extravagant performance. Manners that required self-control in order to maintain quiet within a group and affirm hierarchies do not sit well with this character. Our sources agree that quarrelling, brawling, and even armed confrontations were a part of life in Landsknecht armies. An excessive regard for the sensitivities of others cannot have been common in a violent, masculine subculture where status had to be displayed and honour defended at all cost.

Further, many traditional rules of etiquette simply did not apply. Whether in camps or quarters, Landsknechts rarely ate at shared tables. The opportunity to wash their hands was curtailed by the lack of clean water, and it is unlikely that there was more than the minimum of tableware and cutlery. The finer points of handling serving bowls, saucers, voiders, and manchet bread were a moot point under these circumstances. In addition, the ceremony of dining assumed that there was a host or lord who provided the food and headed the table. Soldiers who purchased their portions from *Sudler* cooks or pooled their resources to cook ate as equals. They owed thanks for their food only to God and themselves. Very likely there was a clear hierarchy in relation to wives, camp followers, and servant boys, but we do not know any details about how it was expressed.

Hygiene

We have already touched on the question of handwashing, but hygiene was a more comprehensive problem for a Landsknecht army. Their commanders were aware of the problem, as is shown by strict instructions to lay out fixed latrines—*Scheißplätze*—that were to be located downstream from where laundry was washed and horses drank. Access to clean water was also important, not so much for the sake of the men as that of the supply train; horses do not drink beer. We know that washing clothes was one of the tasks female camp followers were valued for. Under the circumstances, it is hard to see how it would have been possible to maintain the level of cleanliness expected in a contemporary urban household. Soldiers were dirty, even by the standards of their time.

For our purposes, the question of food hygiene is foremost, of course. Despite all real efforts, this must have been inadequate. Meat was delivered on the hoof and slaughtered fresh, but exposed to heat and flies with inadequate protection and no refrigeration, even a single day was time enough for things to go wrong. We know of no similar regulations covering other foods. Thorough cooking probably provided the only protection against foodborne diseases, a principle that was not understood in theory, but practiced.

Keeping cooking equipment and tableware clean must have represented a challenge of its own. Ideally, an army camp had access to running water, but the riverbank would be crowded with laundresses and grooms with their horses. Heating a cauldron of clean water for the day's dishes, the custom in well-off households, can hardly have been a realistic option. We do not know whether washing dishes was offered as a service the same way laundry was, but either way, a daily procession of camp followers heading for nearby rivers to scrub pots and plates with sand and water must have been a common sight on campaign. As in so many other respects, central organisation could have solved a lot of problems.

Finally, cleanliness of cooking and eating implements, like personal hygiene, was an individual choice made within the context of limited opportunities. Often enough, it would have been less important than other things. Life in the free-market anthill of a Landsknecht camp was challenge enough without worrying how to get the grease out of your bowl.

Recipes

Historical Cooking in Modern Kitchens

The following recipes are based on original sources and adapted to the modern kitchen. Above all, this concerns the tools used in their preparation. We generally no longer use baking pans stood in the embers, few modern ovens allow for spit-roasting, and in place of heavy brass mortars, we use food processors. Of course, the interpretation is also a personal one, mediated through a palate accustomed to modern tastes. That is why each recipe is accompanied by the translated source text it is based on. This leaves the reader the opportunity to decide how far to follow my redaction and where to deviate from it. The quantities, given in metric units and approximate Imperial equivalents, are guidelines, not hard requirements.

Anyone who intensively engages with historical cooking will sooner or later start working with replicas of historical kitchen tools. This takes some practice, but it is a thoroughly enjoyable hobby. This book does not go that far. Here, the focus is on replicating historical flavours using the toolkit of a modern kitchen. The end result is less authentic, but within reach of far more people.

Looking at the tools we need to substitute, the first that comes to mind is the mortar. In the sixteenth century, huge mortars were an indispensable tool in larger kitchens. They were not just used to grind spices, but also to pound nuts, produce meat and vegetable pastes, and even as baking dishes. Electric food processors can replicate many of these functions though the resulting consistency differs.

The process of passing purees through a sieve or cloth, common in the finer cuisine of the time, can also be approximated using a processor, though a stick blender or hand-cranked food mill are adequate for most purposes. Again, the result will not reach the creaminess of anything that was forced through a fine mesh of linen or horsehair, but in most cases it will do fine.

Using a fire to cook also produced different conditions. Cooking pots at the time were mainly ceramic, set near the fire for a slow, even heat. Steel pots set on electric ranges behave very differently. To approximate cooking in pottery, you can slowly raise the temperature and simmer the food on a low setting, or use an electric slow cooker. Metal cauldrons and frying pans, by contrast, would produce a higher, more intense heat over a fire than on an electric stovetop. A gas burner can create a similar heat, though in most cases the difference is not centrally important.

Landsknecht-era cooks had two options to bake things. One was a wood-fired thermal-mass oven into which bread was placed after removing the ashes of the fire.

The other was a closed baking pan that was stood in the embers and had coals heaped on its lid like a Dutch oven. Experienced cooks were able to regulate the heat inside these vessels as precisely the same way we can manage temperatures in a modern oven. Electric or gas ovens are perfectly suitable substitutes for most purposes.

A look at contemporary practice is also useful in choosing ingredients. Few recipes fail to mention spices, often in the formulaic expression *'gutes Gewürz,'* 'good spice'. These recipe collections presupposed a financially potent readership, however. It is likely that Landsknechts, like most poor people, rarely used spices in their daily cooking and would have prepared such dishes without them.

What exactly was meant by *gutes Gewürz* varied by personal inclination and wealth. Pepper, ginger, and cinnamon were relatively affordable at the time while nutmeg, cloves, cardamom, and especially saffron were expensive pleasures and likely limited to the spice boxes of officers' cooks. Native seasonings such as caraway and mustard, on the other hand, were cheap and used with greater abandon.

Another question is to what extent spices then available resembled those we get today. Months of sea and land transport must have been detrimental to their aroma, and vendors were notorious for adulterations. On the other hand, at least in larger kitchens the spices were freshly ground while modern spice powders are often kept for months, bleeding out their flavours. In the end, we simply do not know, and the choice is down to individual taste.

Beer and wine, too, were used both for drinking and cooking, and historical tastes differed from modern ones. Hieronymus Bock describes the ideal wine as a mature, aromatic, rather dry white. Sweet Mediterranean wines and fruit wines, he writes dismissively, were popular with women (Bock LI r). Both *Malvasier* (Malmsey) and *Reinfal* (Ribolla gialla) are still made and resemble their antecedents reasonably closely. Such imports were expensive, though, then more than now, and often enough the choice was made by the purse more than the palate. Domestic production was subject to the vagaries of the weather, and few wines were very aromatic or lasted long. Everyday wine was drunk young, resembling *vin nouveau* or *Federweisser*.

Terroir mattered to the discerning drinker in beer more than wine anyway. Luxury beers like Einbecker, the *Gose* of Goslar, or Hamburg white were traded far. Like modern beers, they were brewed with hops. Medieval *gruit* flavouring was used increasingly rarely. However, the now almost universal Pilsner brewing process was unknown at the time, so if you are looking for authenticity, a lager or Pilsner does not fit well with a Landsknecht meal. A darker mild ale or Altbier most resembles the 'red' barley beer of the time while Einbecker is closest to a dark Bockbier and Hamburg white to a strong Hefeweizen. Nothing like the thirst-quenching small beer of the sixteenth century is brewed in Germany today, and though American 'light' beers are low in alcohol, their flavour profile is completely different. Swedish *lättöl* is still brewed traditionally, as are some 'small beers' by craft brewers. These work well as substitutes.

One final word on ingredient choice: the cuisine of sixteenth-century Germany was heavy and rich by design. Animal protein and fat, sugar, and refined flour demonstrated wealth and enjoyment of the finer things in life. Many portraits of princes show the consequences of these eating habits. Limitations were set by financial circumstances: most people could only afford the richest dishes in small quantities or on special occasions. The recipes in this book should be used similarly. Attempting a low-calorie Landsknecht cuisine misses the point.

Bread: Leavened and Unleavened

The 'daily bread' of the Lord's Prayer was no empty phrase. Especially in the cities, bread was the primary food for most people. On poor tables, it was often enough the only food, but even the richest of meals needed bread to accompany it.

We have no bread recipes surviving from the sixteenth century, but we know from other sources that a great professional bakers produced a great deal of variety. Common bread, sold at regulated prices in city markets, was produced from coarsely bolted flour, water, salt, and leaven. The grain varied by region: rye, wheat, or spelt. By modern standards, this produced a hard and dense bread similar to the crusty loaves still sold by artisanal bakers today. It was sold fresh daily in urban markets, but households that produced their own often stored bread for long periods of time.

We have already touched on the problems posed by supplying an army with bread, and Landsknechts knew how to improvise in times of dearth. Hieronymus Bock writes in the *Teutsche Speißkammer:*

When dearth is abroad, in times of war, and especially when you have to flee, you will not carry much in the way of ovens and kitchenware. You would be glad if you could get flour to cook on hot stones or in the ashes. Experienced soldiers can tell you much about this.

(*Teutsche Speißkammer*, p. XLIV)

Such unleavened flatbreads can be produced in a pan.

45 MINUTES

INGREDIENTS

SIDE DISH FOR 4

- 250 g / 1 ¼ cups flour (coarsely bolted or wholemeal)
- Water
- If desired, butter, oil, or lard

Work the flour and water into a firm, dry dough and knead it thoroughly. Let rest for 30 minutes. Divide into six portions and roll or pat each piece into a flat disc about 2 mm thick.

Heat the pan on the stovetop, and add a small amount of oil or fat if desired. Bake each flatbread for 3–5 minutes, turning over several times to prevent scorching. Serve warm.

Butter and Lard

In a time of growing population and shrinking real wages, meat and fat were increasingly a matter of status. That explains why many recipes use them so generously—they mean to represent wealth. Butter was especially important; combined with bread, it constituted a full meal. In the absence of artificial refrigeration, it had to be preserved for storage, though. It could be salted and the salt washed out with cold water prior to use, or it could be separated from its perishable elements by clarifying it. That is why butterfat or ghee are perfectly acceptable for use in most of our recipes. Fresh, sweet butter as we know it today was considered a delicacy and is often referred to as May butter.

In poorer households, where butter was unaffordable, a greasepot was a central feature of the kitchen. Any fat that was left over during cooking, rendered in frying, or skimmed off soups, was added to it and reused as needed. Hieronymus Bock takes a sanguine view of mixing cheaper fats:

Take three parts of fine, fresh, clean pig lard and two parts of beef tallow melted together and mixed with salt. Poor people can prepare and fatten their soups and dishes with it, it is lovely to use with food.

(*Teutsche Speißkammer*, p. LXXXIIII v)

INGREDIENTS

FOR STORAGE

250 g / 9 oz lard
175 g / 4 ½ oz beef tallow
2 teaspoons salt

20 MINUTES

Melt lard and tallow in a pot on low heat. Mix, add salt, and fill into a ceramic vessel or canning jars. Chill. This fat can be used for frying and added to soups and vegetable dishes. No doubt many Landsknechts knew the taste of relative poverty from their civilian lives.

Cheese Soup

Soup—*Suppe*—was a familiar dish on every table and often the main food of the poor. The term covered more-or-less liquid foods served with bread. Soups could range from delicately spiced almond milk served over sugared white toast to simple vegetable soups served with brown bread from stale loaves soaked to make them palatable. Our sources often mention cheese soup as a hearty, warming meal. There are few recipes for many common dishes, but the *Klosterkochbuch* gives a detailed account of how it was made. Cheese is boiled in broth and beaten into the liquid or passed through a cloth to produce a creamy, viscous consistency.

Pass out cheeses, wash them clean in pure warm water, cut them up small, put them into a pot and set them by the fire with water. Throw in peeled onions, green parsley, the herb and root, and sage leaves. Let that boil well and take care that it does not burn. When it is boiled, pass it through a sieve or cloth and put it back into a clean pot. Make it fat with butter, strew whole caraway on it, salt it, and serve it.

(*Klosterkochbuch*, IV.33)

30 MINUTES

INGREDIENTS

SERVES 4

150 g / 5 oz rich cheese
(e.g., Gouda or Cheddar)

1 parsley root

2 tablespoons chopped parsley

Fresh sage

1 L / 4 cups broth

Salt

Caraway

The cheese can be chosen according to taste. Rich, mature cheeses such as middle-aged Gouda, Cheddar, or Emmental are especially suitable. Processed cheese makes the cooking easier, but is obviously not historically accurate.

Cut the cheese into small pieces or coarsely grind it. Slice the parsley root thinly. Chop the parsley and sage. Bring the broth to a boil and cook the parsley root until soft. Then stir in the parsley and sage and add the cheese. Let everything simmer together for a few minutes, stirring constantly, until the cheese is melted. Pass the soup through a food mill or purée it with an immersion blender. Salt to taste and serve hot, strewn with caraway seeds and accompanied by bread.

SOUP OF GREENS

Krautsuppe

Krautsuppe, a simple soup made with cabbage or other leafy greens, was among the most common kinds of soup eaten. Marx Rumpolt gives a short description of how to make it fit for lordly tables:

Set leafy greens (Kraut) *to cook for a soup, be it cut or chopped, then take whole peppercorns and entire leaves of mace and let it boil with those. When you wish to serve it, take toasted slices of a white wheat bread* (Weck) *or rye bread, fatten it with hot butter and strew it with ginger.*

(Rumpolt, p. CLXII r)

2 HOURS

INGREDIENTS

SERVES 4

500 g / 1 lb white cabbage

1.5 L / 6 cups meat or vegetable stock

Mace

Peppercorns

Coarsely chop the cabbage. Set to cook with the stock in a large pot and gently simmer for 75–90 minutes until soft. Add entire mace leaves and peppercorns for a luxurious version (leave out spices for a poor dish). Add more liquid if necessary.

This soup can easily be made in a pressure cooker. The cooking time is reduced to about 30 minutes at the vegetable setting.

Serve with toasted bread and butter.

A *Krautsuppe* could have meat, bacon, roots, or other vegetables added to it if it was meant to make an entire meal. Rumpolt's recipe is intended to be served as part of a menu.

Pea Soup

Pea soup was another simple, universally familiar dish variations of which were eaten across the social spectrum. It was hot, filling, easy to prepare, and easy to keep hot. Balthasar Staindl provides a recipe, though it is clearly adjusted to the desires of his wealthy readership.

Clear pea soup: Boil the peas, take off only the clear broth, chop onions very finely, colour it yellow, season it, and take fat, mace, and toasted white wheat bread with it. [...] but if you make it thick, you lightly purée the peas (through a cloth), add fried, cut onions, colour it yellow, and season it. It must be stirred vigorously and, if desired, passed through a cloth.

(Staindl, #256)

The thick soup described in the second part is probably closer to what was commonly served in peasant households, though without the saffron and spices. Steady and vigorous stirring is needed to prevent it from sticking to the pot, especially when it is cooked over a fire.

INGREDIENTS

SERVES 4

24 HOURS SOAKING TIME, 1 HOUR COOKING TIME

- 500 g / 1 lb split peas
- Water
- 1.5 L / 6 cups meat or vegetable stock
- 2 onions
- 2 tablespoons lard or butter
- Salt
- Vinegar
- Spices

Soak the peas overnight. Discard soaking water, set to cook with the stock and simmer for 60 minutes until soft. Shortly before they are finished, finely chop the onions and sauté them in the fat. Add to the soup and mash or purée everything together. Season with salt, vinegar, and spices as desired. Mace fits well. Serve hot over toasted bread.

Bacon, sausage, or different vegetables can be added to pea soup, and this very likely happened in poorer households where it served as an entire meal. In wealthier homes, the soup was only part of a meal and accordingly prepared more plainly.

Mus

The most humble of foods was *Mus*, often cooked individually in small pots. This usually referred to a grain-based porridge, but could include any food cooked to a spoonable mush. Contemporary paintings of the Nativity typically include Joseph cooking *Mus* for Mary over a small fire. Landsknechts, too, likely ate grain porridge more often than they would have liked. The ingredients were easily portable, the dish flexible and simple to make. Many recipes for cereal *Mus* survive, but most of them deal with ways of adding to the appeal of the basic version. Balthasar Staindl instructs us:

Take oatmeal or flour, cook it in hot fat, stir it together and add water or meat broth or pea broth. You can also make it with pea flour.

(Staindl, #270)

This is probably the standard way of making small portions. Quickly frying the grains in fat before boiling raises the flavour and adds roasting aromas. Larger quantities could not be made this way, though. They were cooked in large ports directly in liquid.

CEREAL MUS

20 MINUTES

INGREDIENTS

SERVES 4

2 tablespoons lard or butter

250 g / 2 cups oatmeal

1 L / 4 cups meat or vegetable stock

Melt the fat in the bottom of a saucepan and quickly sauté the oatmeal. Add the stock and bring to a simmer. Cook till done on low heat, stirring regularly.

This recipe works for all kinds of grains and can use milk or wine (or plain water) in place of stock. The finished dish can be enriched with eggs, butter, sugar, or spices. Milk *Mus* was served with *Triget* (see p. 128).

BREAD MUS

Travellers in a hurry or carrying little cooking equipment could also opt for a bread-based version. The easiest way was probably simply soaked grated bread served cold. The *Klosterkochbuch* described how this was done with beer.

Grate stale bread, add it to beer, not too thick nor too runny. Add ground caraway, anise, and coriander, and a little sugar or honey. Stir it together quickly and serve it.

(*Klosterkochbuch*, IV.55)

More detailed instructions are not really needed here, though it is unlikely most Landsknechts would season their beer *Mus* with anise, coriander, or sugar. Instructions for an enriched and cooked version is described by Sabina Welser:

A good Mus *of white wheat bread: Take grated white wheat bread, stir it in a pan with meat broth and let boil well together so that it becomes soft* (musig). *Then take four egg yolks beaten with cold meat broth and let that boil together.*

(Sabina Welser, #127)

INGREDIENTS

SERVES 4

750 ml / 3 cups meat stock
4 egg yolks
250 g / 2 cups breadcrumbs
Salt or butter if desired

15 MINUTES

Reserve two ladles of the stock and beat with the egg yolks. Bring the rest to a rolling boil in a saucepan and gradually stir in the breadcrumbs. Simmer on low heat until smooth and creamy, then stir in the egg yolks and allow to set. Add salt and/or butter, if desired, and serve hot.

Curly Mus

Pasta dishes were already well known in South Germany by the sixteenth century. Many cookbooks include recipes for some form of noodles cooked in milk or stock and served in soup, as a side dish, or as a main course. Most of them require more time, effort, and equipment than the average camp follower or *Sudler* cook likely would have had or bothered with, though. An interesting reference in the *Kuchenmaistrey* mentions a *Zotten Mües*, a curly porridge, which is detailed in an earlier fifteenth-century manuscript from Austria. It describes a method of preparing hand-pulled noodles that could be accommodated by the limited means of a camp kitchen and was familiar enough around 1490 to not need any definition.

Take good white wheat flour, make a dough with egg whites and have boiling milk ready in a pan. Take the dough and pluck it into the milk in small pieces while it boils. It is to be salted beforehand. Also add fat. See that it stays worm-shaped, do not oversalt it, and serve it.

(Dorotheenkloster MS, #150)

Balthasar Staindl's *Kochbuch* of 1569 includes a similar recipe, but here the dough is rolled out and cut into irregular pieces. This seems to have become standard in upper-class cuisine at the time—shaping noodles by hand was now considered lower-class. Staindl's version also uses sugar instead of salt.

INGREDIENTS

SERVES 4

30 MINUTES

5–6 eggs (or 10 egg whites)
500 g / 3 ½ cups flour
1 L / 4 cups milk
Salt
Butter

Work eggs and flour into a stiff, dry dough and shape into a ball. This can be done a day in advance. Lightly salt the milk and bring to a boil in a sufficiently large pot to accommodate the swelling noodles. Tear pieces off the ball of dough and add to the boiling milk until it is all used up. Leave to cook over low heat until soft, then add a little butter and serve.

Eier im Schmalz

Eggs, nourishing, easily stored, and versatile, were universally popular. Egg dishes, often easy and quick to prepare, were part of everyday food. The simplest approaches were to drink eggs raw or cook them in the embers of the fire, but our sources also mention poached and scrambled eggs. Recipes for such basic dishes are almost non-existent, they were too familiar to require instruction. The popular *Eier im Schmalz*, eggs fried in fat, are equally rarely described, though Staindl includes a recipe:

Break an egg into a bowl, salt it, and strew a little flour on it. Take fat into a pan and let it get very hot. Put in the egg, fry it, turn it over so that it turns brown, and serve it either dry or in a sauce of apples.

(Staindl, #208)

The *Kunstbuch von mancherlei Essen* by Franz de Rontzier also mentions fried eggs. He suggests adding rosemary or sage to the pan and to serve the finished eggs with either salt and pepper or with parmesan cheese. Apple sauce (see p. 122) as suggested by Staindl also fits, though.

INGREDIENTS

INGREDIENTS PER PERSON

1 teaspoon lard or butter
Rosemary or sage, if desired
2 eggs
Salt
Flour

5 MINUTES

Heat the fat in a pan (use more than we would for modern fried eggs) and add rosemary or sage, if desired. Break each egg carefully into a small bowl, leaving the yolk intact. Lightly salt the eggs and dust with flour, then gently slide them into the hot fat one by one. Turn over once the white has solidified and finish frying on the other side.

EIERKUCHEN

Eierkuchen

Several recipes in Franz de Rontzier describe *Eierkuchen*, a kind of omelette or Spanish tortilla with various added ingredients. The instructions are not detailed, but fairly intuitive and quite tasty. Along with the rustic version involving bacon, apples, and onions, the book also mentions *Eierkuchen* made with salmon, kipper, raisins, and parmesan cheese.

You fry lean bacon with onions and apples, break eggs upon it, and let it fry.

(de Rontzier, p. 535)

10 MINUTES

INGREDIENTS

INGREDIENTS PER PERSON

50 g / 2 oz bacon
½ apple
½ onion
Fat for frying
2 eggs

Cube the bacon and apple. Slice the onion into fine rings. Quickly sauté all together in a hot pan, then add the eggs. Reduce the heat, cover the pan, and cook until done without stirring.

When cooking *Eierkuchen* with fish, you should take care to break it up in the pan before adding the eggs. Parmesan is best added along with the eggs, in small lumps, so that it does not melt entirely before the egg hardens.

FRENCH TOAST

Arme Ritter

Arme Ritter ('poor knights'), a version of French toast, is another dish with a long history that is mentioned occasionally but almost never described in detail. Franz de Rontzier includes short instructions to prepare what was a universally familiar treat in his day. Mace, though, was probably not used in most common kitchens.

Arme Ritter *of white bread*

You cut white wheat bread in slices or rounds, lay it in eggs that were beaten with mace, and fry it in butter. The white bread is also first soaked in milk and then fried in butter with eggs.

(de Rontzier, p. 527)

INGREDIENTS

SERVES 4

10 MINUTES

- 6 eggs
- Mace, if desired
- 4 thick slices of dry white bread
- Butter for frying

Beat the eggs in a deep plate or dish. Add mace, if desired. Successively soak the bread slices in the beaten egg and fry in the butter at a gentle heat. This goes well with *Triget* (see p. 128) or a fruit sauce.

Mustard Eggs

Along with a plethora of courtly egg dishes, Marx Rumpolt also records a simple preparation of hard-boiled eggs fried with mustard. This hot, rich, savoury dish must have appealed to hungry Landsknechts and is certainly no invention of Rumpolt.

Take eggs that are hard-boiled and shelled cleanly. Cut them in quarters or into thin rounds. Take butter in a pan, heat it, and throw in the hard eggs. Fry them well in the butter and do not oversalt them. Add sour mustard that is made with vinegar, toss it around the pan with the mustard two or three times, and serve it hot. Thus it is good and tasty.

(Rumpolt, p. CXLVI v)

INGREDIENTS

INGREDIENTS PER PERSON

3 hard-boiled eggs
1 tablespoon butter
2 tablespoons mustard

10 MINUTES

Shell eggs and cut into pieces. Melt butter in a pan and quickly sauté the eggs. Add mustard and stir till all coated. Serve hot with bread.

Bread Pancakes

Pancakes were another popular and appealing method of turning eggs into a meal. Along with a simple batter, our sources include several recipes that use grated or cut dry bread to make pancakes. The cookbooks ennoble this common fare with expensive ingredients, but they must have existed also without the addition of spices and dried fruit. Balthasar Staindl describes their preparation very clearly:

Take hard pieces of white wheat bread and pound them small. Take of these as much as you please. Break eggs into it, salt it, and also add many raisins. When it stands a while, the bread draws the eggs into itself and dries. Then break more eggs into it so that it acquires the correct thickness and then drop it into the fat in the way of pancakes. It must not be too hot. Move the pan about so they rise. Serve a yellow pepper sauce or an almond sauce over such cakes, or a sauce of apples, and season the sauce.

(Staindl, #203)

30 MINUTES

INGREDIENTS

SERVES 4

250 g / 8 oz dry white bread
6–8 eggs
Salt
Milk if needed
Fat for frying

Break or grind up the bread (older recipes often stipulate bread chunks rather than small crumbs) and place in a bowl. Break 6 eggs into the bowl and stir. Salt to taste. Let the batter stand for ten minutes and add more eggs or thin with milk if necessary. It should be thick, but not dry. Heat fat in a pan, cut out small portions of the batter with a spoon and drop into the pan. Fry for 8–10 minutes, turning over once. If the batter is chunky, they often need to be pressed flat with a ladle or spatula. Serve hot, e.g., with apple sauce (see p. 122) or *Triget* (see p. 128).

Pea Fritters

This recipe from the *Kuchenmaistrey* turns common peas into an attractive main dish that—without meat, egg, or dairy—is suitable for Lent. Pious Landsknechts keeping the fast must have found such things interesting.

Make good fritters from another part of the peas thus: Strew the hand with flour and shape the fritters. Make a batter from yellow-coloured wine and coat the fritters in it. Lift them out with a spoon into the pan and fry as many as you wish.

(*Kuchenmaistrey*, 2. LVIII-LXI)

INGREDIENTS

SIDE DISH FOR 4

200 g / 7 oz split peas
Salt
Water
Breadcrumbs if needed
Saffron, if desired
250 ml / 1 cup white wine
150 g / 1¼ cups flour
Fat for deep-frying
Extra flour to work the fritters

2 HOURS

Cook the split peas in lightly salted water and drain well. Purée or mash the peas. The purée should be stiff enough to shape small dumplings with a spoon. If it is too thin, adding breadcrumbs can help the consistency. Salt to taste.

Dissolve a small amount of saffron in the wine and beat with the flour to make a thin batter. Salt to taste. Heat fat to deep-fry.

Carefully shape walnut-sized dumplings from the pea purée with floured hands. Carefully turn them over in the batter with a fork and immediately slide them into the hot fat. Fry for 3–5 minutes. Serve warm.

The *Kuchenmaistrey* suggests serving these fritters either in a sweet spice sauce on a wine basis or in a roux-based pepper sauce. As a third option, they are to be served with fried apple slices and honey. To prepare these, peel and core an apple, cut it into thin wedges, coat them in any leftover batter and fry them after the pea fritters are done. Drizzle with honey before serving.

Dried Pears in Pepper Sauce

Dried pears were prepared in autumn to store over the year. The *Kuchenmaistrey* contains an interesting recipe describing how to prepare them in a spicy bread-bound sauce called a *Pfeffer*. The text states this is a dish for poor people, but it was most likely altered to meet the expectations of the wealthy. Ginger, at least, was not likely something cottagers and labourers enjoyed much.

Eating such pears in a bread pepper sauce is good food for poor people. Rye bread grated in and eaten, it nourishes well and strengthens a bad stomach. It is made only with salt and pure ginger, only with wine and vinegar.

(*Kuchenmaistrey*, i. XXIII)

INGREDIENTS

SERVES 4

300 g / 10 oz dried pears
Water
250 ml / 1 cup white wine
100 g / 1 cup grated dark rye bread
Vinegar
Salt
Ginger

24 HOURS SOAKING TIME, 45 MINUTES COOKING

Soak the dried pears overnight, barely covered in water. On the next day, place them in a pot with the wine and add of the water they soaked in until they are fully covered. Simmer at low heat until soft and carefully lift the pears out of the liquid with a slotted spoon. Then gradually add the grated bread to the cooking liquid, stirring the entire time. The sauce can now be puréed or passed through a food-mill to achieve a smooth, thick consistency. Season to taste with salt, vinegar, and ginger and return the pears to the sauce. Serve hot.

In a truly poor household, both ginger and wine would have been luxury goods. Modern tastes may prefer to sweeten this dish with honey.

It is not easy to come by dried pears these days. You can produce them yourself, though. Select firm, aromatic ones (ideally cooking pears, but no soft, juicy ones). Quarter and core them, then lay them out on a wire rack with the skin side down. Dry overnight in an oven set at 75°C / 170°F. Keep the oven door slightly ajar by wedging a wooden spoon into it to allow the moisture out. The following morning, lay out the quarters on a radiator or string them on yarn and hang them up to dry out completely.

Roast

Roasting spits are a regular feature in pictures of Landsknecht camps and we know that fresh meat was sold in camp markets. In most urban marketplaces, the most prized and expensive kind of meat was *Brät*, the pieces suitable for roasting. Very likely this was the same here.

Roasts were prepared on a spit at some distance from the fire while being basted regularly. The contemporary term is 'cool' roasting. It was a demanding skill, but common enough for almost no detailed descriptions to survive. We know from various sources that lean meat was basted with butter or other kinds of fat while fat meat was basted with salt water. The *Klosterkochbuch* has a good description of preparing a simple roast.

Take the roast, beat it soft and salt it. Let it thus lie a day and a night, then stick it on a spit and set it by the fire with a small pot of salt water. Baste it (while it is) hot with that so that it roasts half done, and afterwards, when it is all done, serve it.
(*Klosterkochbuch*, III.27)

2½ HOURS

INGREDIENTS

SERVES 4

1 kg / 2 lbs roasting meat
For lean meat:
125 g / 4 oz melted butter
For fat meat:
500 ml / 2 cups salt water
Salt

Imitating a spit roast in a modern kitchen is not easy. A free-swinging barbecue grill works well if the meat is turned over regularly. When using a conventional oven, a closed roasting pan helps. Of course, if you do have the opportunity, using an actual spit is best.

Preheat the oven to 150°C / 300°F. Place the meat in a roasting pan and either rub it with salt and butter, or moisten it with salt water. Slowly roast in a closed roasting pan and baste every 10–15 minutes, also using the juices collecting in the roasting pan. After 2 hours, increase the heat to 180°C / 350°F and finish the meat in an open roasting pan, basting frequently to prevent it drying out.

It was customary to place pottery basting pans under roasting spits to catch the juices and fat dripping down. This was used to baste the meat, and vegetables could also be cooked slowly in it to be served alongside the roast. If the roasting pan is large enough, vegetables can be arranged around and under the meat to be cooked in a similar fashion.

Hungarian Roast

Marx Rumpolt also includes a recipe for a garlic-marinated roast he calls Hungarian. The ingredients would have been available and since garlic was associated with peasant food, this would also fit the proletarian image of common Landsknecht soldiers.

Take beef roast and marinate it overnight. Take half vinegar and half water for the liquid, and with that pounded garlic and a little salt. Let the roast lie in it overnight. In the morning, take it out of the marinade, salt it, stick it on the spit, and roast it. Take the marinade that the roast has lain in, pour it off so that the solids stay at the bottom (of the bowl), put it into a tinned fish kettle with a little ground pepper and unmelted butter and let it boil. Set it under the roast in a tinned pan and baste it with that. This is a good dish for Polish and Hungarian gentlemen.

(Rumpolt, p. XLV)

INGREDIENTS

SERVES 4

For the marinade:

250 ml / 1 cup white wine vinegar
250 ml / 1 cup water
2 bulbs garlic
Salt

1 kg / 2 lbs beef roast
Salt
50 g / 5 tablespoons butter
Pepper

24 HOURS SOAKING TIME, 2 HOURS COOKING

The previous day, mix vinegar and water in a bowl. Peel and crush garlic and add to the marinade with about a tablespoon of salt. Pierce the roast all around with a small, pointy knife and leave it in the marinade overnight.

The next day, preheat the oven to 175°C / 350°F. Remove the roast from the marinade, rub it with salt and place it in a roasting pan. Strain the marinade into a steel saucepan and bring to a boil with the butter and some pepper. Bake the roast for 90–100 minutes in a closed roasting pan, regularly basting with the marinade.

Originally, such a roast would have been roasted on a spit by the fire and basted from a dripping pan placed below it that would catch the juices falling from the meat.

Boiled Mutton in Vinegar

This recipe is at odds with modern expectations of how to serve meat, but it is actually quite good served for lunch with bread and butter, or as a cold main dish in summertime. Of course, at the time it would more likely have come to the table in autumn, when aged sheep were slaughtered. Similar sauces made with chives or different herbs were also served with boiled beef.

Take the shoulder from a sheep's quarter and boil it entire, the way you boil other meat. When it is boiled, lay it out to cool. Then take parsley greens, cut it up small, grind it in a mortar, pour in vinegar, leave it standing half an hour or an hour, then press out the same parsley through a nice cloth and put into the expressed liquid ground ginger and ground pepper, then pour it over the abovementioned shoulder and serve it cold as a dish.

(Staindl, #170)

INGREDIENTS

SERVES 4

- 1 kg / 2 lbs mutton (shoulder or leg, more if many bones are included)
- Salt
- Possibly mirepoix
- 250 ml / 1 cup white wine vinegar
- 2 bunches parsley
- Ginger
- Pepper

2–3 HOURS

Wash the mutton and truss it up if necessary. Gently simmer it in a pot covered with salted water for 90–120 minutes until completely cooked. The flavour is improved by adding root vegetables such as mirepoix.

While the meat is cooking, process the vinegar with the parsley until no more pieces are visible. Let settle for 15 minutes and strain through a sieve, taking care to press out as much liquid as possible. Season to taste with salt, pepper, and ginger.

Remove the meat from the pot and let cool. Slice and arrange in a deep serving bowl. Pour over the parsley vinegar and let stand for at least 30 minutes before serving. This dish can be made several days beforehand and kept refrigerated.

Boiled Meat

Sudler did most business in freshly slaughtered meat boiled in their large cauldrons. Many households, too, served boiled meat more often than roasted. Recipes or detailed descriptions are rare, most likely because this, too, was a matter of course: boil cauldron, add meat, done. The recipe in the *Klosterkochbuch* also pays more attention to the sauce than the cooking process:

Take beef that is good, boil it so that it is done. Then take chives as much as you think good, grind them small, and dissolve them in sour wine or vinegar. When the meat is cooked, pour that over it, and remember the salt.

(*Klosterkochbuch*, III.23)

It is not really that simple. Boiling meat tender takes skill. Today, most meat is not sold freshly slaughtered, but matured for at least several days. Accordingly, it needs to be cooked more slowly to prevent it from becoming too tough. All cuts suitable for boiling will work for this dish. South German boiled beef today uses *Tafelspitz*, a section of the topside. If in doubt, a roasting-grade cut will likely perform better than stewing beef.

2 HOURS

INGREDIENTS

SERVES 4

- 1.5 kg / 3 lbs lower-grade roast or stewing beef
- Water
- Salt
- Marrowbones, if desired
- Root vegetables or mirepoix, if desired
- Onions, if desired

Place the meat in a pot with lightly salted boiling water, reduce the heat, and simmer for about 2 hours, skimming occasionally. To prevent the meat from sticking to the bottom, small wooden skewers or marrowbones can be placed under it. Test for doneness with a small vegetable knife or metal skewer: the meat is done when it can be pierced through easily. Cut and serve hot with a sauce.

At the time, vegetables were often cooked along with the meat in the same cauldron or pot. Adding some coarsely chopped onions or mirepoix to the pot improves the flavour of the meat even if you do not serve them alongside afterwards. If you want to serve the vegetables, it is best to only add them for the last 30 minutes.

Pan-Fried Meat

Another way of preparing fresh meat was to sauté it in a pan and then slowly finish it in broth. Compared to boiling, that was a rather extravagant approach, but the often highly seasoned dishes of this kind were well suited to raising thirst. Balthasar Staindl describes a simple preparation:

Also take the thick roasting meat of a calf or a young sheep and cut off thin slices with a knife, one finger long and two fingers wide. Beat them with the back of a knife. Take a proper amount of fat in a pan, let it get hot and put in the meat. Let it fry for a long time. When it has fried for a good while, add a swig of vinegar and meat broth. If the broth is already salted, add only a little salt to the pan or it is easily oversalted. Before you pour it in, take clove powder and season it so that it turns black. Let it boil so long that it becomes tender. It acquires a fine, thick sauce. Serve it on a platter, it is good.

(Staindl, #166)

INGREDIENTS

SERVES 4

45-60 MINUTES

750 g / 1½ lbs roasting beef, veal, or lamb
4 tablespoons lard or butterfat
Vinegar
500 ml / 2 cups meat stock
Salt
Spices to taste (cloves go better with lamb than veal or beef)

Cut the meat into 7 cm x 4 cm strips and beat them tender with a mallet or the back of a large knife. Heat the fat in a deep-frying pan or cast-iron skillet and sauté the meat at high heat, stirring constantly. When the meat is browned all around and starts sweating juices, add a generous dash of vinegar and the meat stock. Salt and season to taste, then simmer at low heat until the meat is tender and the liquid reduced by at least two thirds. This can take an hour or longer. Serve hot with bread and butter.

VENISON IN PEPPER SAUCE

Wildpfeffer

Meat was often served 'in a *Pfeffer*' i.e., a pepper sauce, a familiar process rarely described in detail. This unusually precise recipe from Sabina Welser is for venison, but poultry or rabbit was also prepared this way.

To cook venison in a pepper sauce
Boil fresh venison in two parts of water and one part of wine. When it is cooked, cut it in pieces, lay it in a pepper sauce and let it boil in that for a while. Make the sauce thus: Take rye bread, cut off the hard crust and cut the bread in pieces as thick as a finger and as wide as the loaf itself is. Toast those over a fire until both ends begin turning black. Then lay them in cold water, do not leave it in there long. Then place it in a cauldron, add all the broth in which the venison was boiled, and pass that through a cloth. Chop onions and bacon very small, fry it thoroughly together, and do not add too little to the pepper sauce. Season it well, let it boil down together and add vinegar, thus you have a good pepper sauce.
(Sabina Welser, #4)

1 HOUR OR MORE

INGREDIENTS

SERVES 4

750 g / 1½ lbs meat in chunks (e.g., stewing venison)
250 ml / 1 cup wine
Water
2 thick slices dark rye bread, crust removed
100 g / 4 oz bacon
2 onions
Salt
Pepper and other spices as desired
Vinegar

Place the meat in a pot, pour in the wine and add water until covered. Gently simmer until the meat is tender. Depending on the type of meat used, the time needed can vary.

Toast the bread and briefly soak it in cold water. Finely dice the bacon and onions.

Remove the meat from the broth and reserve. Quickly sauté the bacon and onions in a saucepan and add the broth. Then add the bread slices, briefly bring everything to a boil, and purée the sauce. Season to taste with salt, pepper, and vinegar. Similar recipes also mention ginger, saffron, nutmeg, and mace. Add the meat, return to a simmer, and serve hot.

FÜRHESS

Fürhess

A *Fürhess* was a small dish made from the less desirable parts of small animals. It could use poultry, rabbits, or other animals when the meatier parts were needed for dishes enjoying higher status. The most important other ingredient was the blood of the freshly slaughtered animal, a fact that poses a problem for replicating it. Some traditional butchers still sell fresh blood, mainly pig, that can be used. The *Innsbrucker Kochbuch* broadly describes the preparation.

If you would make a Fürhess, *boil the meat and chop it, then pour in the blood with wine or vinegar. Grate bread into it and honey. Also add spices and finely chopped onion, and add fat. Prepare it thus and salt it etc.*

(Innsbruck MS, #37)

Different recipes add details such as that the onion is fried, and some include apples as another common ingredient.

INGREDIENTS

SIDE DISH FOR 4

- 400 g / 1 lb meat (any kind)
- Water
- Salt
- 1 onion
- 1 apple, if desired
- Lard or butter
- 250 ml / 1 cup fresh blood
- Salt
- Honey
- Vinegar
- Breadcrumbs if needed

1½ HOURS

This dish can be prepared well with the bonier, less popular cuts such as chicken backs, pig's trotters, or the forelegs of rabbits. They are boiled in salted water, the meat pulled off the bones and coarsely chopped. Reserve the cooking liquid.

Finely dice the onion and, if desired, the apple. Heat fat in a deep pan or cast-iron skillet and sauté the onion and apple, then add the meat. Slowly pour in the blood, stirring constantly until it begins to thicken. Then stir in a little of the broth and bring to a simmer. Season to taste with salt, vinegar, and honey. If necessary, thicken with breadcrumbs.

A *Fürhess* can also be prepared directly in a pot by stirring the blood into boiling broth. That method easily causes lumps to form, though.

Bratwurst

The most coveted kind of sausage was *Bratwurst*, made from sheer, roasting-grade muscle meat rather than offal. Sabina Welserin records a recipe for these, and it is very much worth trying out if you feel up to the challenge. Making sausages would have been a butcher's job, not something most home cooks did.

If you want to make good Bratwurst
Take four pounds of pork and four pounds of beef, have it chopped small, then take two pounds of bacon into it and chop it together. Add about three Seidel *of water, and also add salt and pepper, as you like to eat it, or if you like to have herbs in it, you can take a little a little sage and a little marjoram, and you will have good* Bratwurst.

(Sabina Welser, #25)

1 HOUR

INGREDIENTS

SERVES 4

- 400 g / 1 lb pork
- 400 g / 1 lb beef
- 200 g / ½ lb fat bacon
- Ice water
- Salt
- Pepper
- Sage
- Marjoram
- Sausage skins

Unless you are very patient, this recipe needs either a meat grinder or a powerful food processor. Finely grind the pork, beef, and bacon and mix all three quickly, making sure the meat stays cold. Add iced water until the mass can be passed through a funnel. Season to taste with salt, pepper, sage, and marjoram.

Slide the sausage skin over a funnel and tie off the end. Stuff the filling through the funnel, pushing with your thumb as you support the sausages with your other hand. Some meat grinders have a sausage filling attachment that can help with this. Tie off sausages about 15 cm in length. Cook them on a grill or in the oven at 180°C / 375°F until fully done. Serve hot, with mustard (see p. 127) or apple sauce (see p. 122).

If you have the equipment, smoking improves the flavour of these sausages considerably. They can also be cooked on a baking sheet without a casing, similar to breakfast sausages.

FILLED STOMACH (MEAT PUDDING)

Filled Stomach

Meat puddings were part of what butchers produced from freshly slaughtered animals. In contemporary German, they were classed as sausages. At the time, they would have been made with a fresh stomach or large intestine. Today, these are hard to come by. We substitute a greased and floured pudding cloth or tin pudding basin. Such dishes were traditional slaughter day treats, and since every day was slaughter day in an army camp, the ingredients were available daily.

Fill the stomach thus: Take chopped pork, eggs, cut white bread, fat meat, pepper, caraway, saffron, and salt. Mix it all together and fill the stomach with it not too full. Boil it fresh. When it is boiled, remove the filling from the stomach, cut the stomach in four pieces and chop it with eggs.

(Maister Hans, #65)

1½ HOURS

INGREDIENTS

SERVES 4

100 g / 4 oz fatback or pork fat
750 g / 1½ lbs ground pork
2 eggs
200 g / 2–2½ cups cubed dry bread or coarse breadcrumbs
Pepper
Caraway
Salt
Saffron if desired
Butter
Flour

Finely dice fatback and knead into a filling with the ground pork, eggs, and bread. Season with pepper, caraway, and salt. Saffron is for upper-class cooking.

Lay out a pudding cloth or clean, undamaged dish towel on a working surface. Grease with butter and dust with flour. Work the meat into a sausage shape, lay on the cloth lengthwise, and roll up carefully. Tie off both ends tightly with string.

Carefully lower the meat pudding into a large pot of boiling water and simmer for 45–60 minutes. Lift out with two slotted spoons, let the excess water drain off and lay out on a work surface. Cut off the strings with scissors and unroll carefully. Slice and serve hot with bread and a sauce.

This dish can also be prepared in a pudding basin.

Stuffed Cabbage

This recipe exemplifies the playful attitude to cookery that is prevalent in many of the sixteenth-century recipe collections. A *Sudler* cook might well have made it to impress customers in autumn when cabbage was in season.

Prepare it thus: Take good, firm cabbage heads, cut off a broad slice on the stalk side, and hollow them out inside so that they stay whole. Then take roasting-grade meat of lambs, calves, or pigs that is not old, chop it very fine, and add fat meat that must not be chopped too fine. Break eggs into it, add raisins, and fill it into the cabbage. Put the slice back on the cabbage head and fix it with skewers. Sauté it well, like any potherb, then drain the fat and pour pork broth over it. Boil it well and see that it does not burn. When you serve it, take cream that is sour. Cut open the cabbage heads in the serving bowl, that way you see the filling inside the cabbage. Some make scrambled egg with raisins and fill that into the cabbage.

(Staindl, #221)

3 HOURS

INGREDIENTS

SERVES 4

- 1 medium-sized head of white cabbage
- 1 kg / 2 lbs ground meat (pork or veal)
- 3–4 eggs
- 200 g / 7 oz raisins
- 100 g / 4 oz finely chopped fatback or pork fat
- Salt
- Fat for frying
- 2–3 L / 8–12 cups meat stock
- 250 ml / 1 cup sour cream

Strip the cabbage head of its outermost leaves and wash it. Cut off a slice about 1–2 fingers thick at the bottom end and set it aside. Carefully hollow out the cabbage head. Knead the ground meat, eggs, raisins, and fatback into a filling. Salt to taste. Fill the cabbage head, replace the slice taken off and secure with toothpicks and string. Tie a loop to the knot to lift the head out of the pot after boiling.

Heat fat in a large pot. Sauté the cabbage head from all sides, turning it carefully so as not to break it. Fill up with meat stock and simmer 2–3 hours.

Heat the sour cream in a saucepan just before serving, salt to taste, and pour over the cabbage in the serving bowl.

Boiled Chicken

Chickens were served both roasted and boiled. Staindl includes instructions for a simple and attractive way of preparing boiled chickens with a bread-thickened sauce similar to the one used for *Wildpfeffer*.

Prepare the chickens nicely and cleanly, place them in a pot, pour in wine and meat broth, salt it in measure, colour it yellow, and season it not too much. Prepare the broth for this and if you want to have the sauce thick, take two toasted slices of white wheat bread, lay them in with the boiling chickens and mash them so that they soften. Take out the boiled bread slices and the livers, pound them, and pass them through together with spices. Pour that back in with the chickens and let them finish cooking.

(Staindl, #172)

45 MINUTES

INGREDIENTS

SERVES 4

- 4 chicken legs or one entire chicken
- 250 ml / 1 cup white wine
- Meat stock
- Spices as desired (saffron for upper-class cooking)
- 2 thick slices of white bread
- 1 chicken liver

Wash the chicken legs and place them in a pot. If an entire chicken is prepared, quarter it. Add the wine and fill up with meat stock until the meat is just covered. Season to taste (just pepper for a plain version; saffron, ginger, and mace, e.g., for a luxurious one). Bring to a slow boil and simmer for about 15 minutes in a closed pot.

Lightly toast the bread, but do not burn it. Add the slices to the pot with the liver. Continue cooking for another 5 minutes, then remove the chicken with a slotted spoon and purée the cooking liquid with the bread and liver. Adjust salt and spices, return the cooked chicken to the sauce and heat through once more. Serve hot.

Staindl writes in recipe #189 that boiled chickens were customarily served with bread and grated cheese, but a grain porridge also goes well with this dish.

ROAST CHICKEN IN THE GERMAN STYLE

Roast Chicken

Roast chickens are mentioned in many Landsknecht songs and we can assume that they were also popular in reality. They were kept in most rural households for eggs, and transporting one, unlike a cow or pig, required little organisation or effort. They could also be gutted and roasted with very basic equipment. Contemporary sources distinguish between preparing roast chickens in the German style, filled with eggs and meat, and in the Italian style, with herbs. The *Kuchenmaistrey* gives us a recipe for the former:

If you would boil or roast or fill a good chicken, prepare the chicken nicely and gut it. Scrape the guts clean. Take the head and neck, the liver, stomach, and all intestines and boil it in a pot or a pan. Chop it well with parsley, break raw eggs into it, season it and salt it. Chop aged bacon into it and small raisins or roasted pears. Knead it well together, that is the filling.

(*Kuchenmaistrey*, 2. III)

Aside from the raisins and unspecified spices, this could have been prepared from basic ingredients in camp.

2½ HOURS

INGREDIENTS

SERVES 4

- 1 roasting chicken with innards
- Salt
- 2–3 small pears (cooking pears, if possible)
- 2 eggs
- Spices as desired

Chickens with their innards are sometimes sold frozen, otherwise ordered from traditional butchers. They usually include only the neck, liver, stomach, and kidneys, but that is quite adequate for this recipe.

Preheat the oven to 150°C / 300°F. Wash the chicken, pat it dry and rub with salt inside and out. Boil the innards in salted water, pick the meat off the bones of the neck and chop or coarsely process it together with the other organ meats. Quarter and core the pears and cook them in the oven. This can be done during the preheating. Mash the pears, mix them with the meat, add eggs and salt, and season to taste (pepper harmonises well).

Stuff the chicken and sew the body cavity shut. Cook in a closed roasting pan for 90 minutes, then remove the lid and brown at 180°C / 375°F for 20–30 minutes. Serve hot.

Chicken with Lettuce

Several recipes mention chickens boiled with lettuce. Using lettuce as a potherb sounds strange to us today, but it actually works well. Anna Wecker writes that it should be mixed with spinach and chard whilst Maria Stengler suggests using lettuce only. It is likely that any potherb would do in simpler kitchens. Sabina Welser describes the technique best:

If you would make chickens in lettuce, take a pot and lay in a handful of lettuce leaves and place a chicken on that, again a handful of lettuce and again a chicken on top and so forth. Then take good meat broth that is fat and add a good lump of butter, salt it, and boil it until it has boiled enough. Add a little mace. You must take the lettuce and wash it thoroughly beforehand. That is how it is made.

(Sabina Welser, #90)

1 HOUR

INGREDIENTS

SERVES 4

- 4 chicken legs or breasts (if possible lean, from heirloom landraces)
- 1 head of lettuce
- Meat stock
- Mace
- 1–2 tablespoons butter (less if the meat is fatty already)

Wash and pat dry the chicken pieces. Remove the large leaves from the lettuce, wash thoroughly and dry. Place a generous layer of leaves on the bottom of a tall pot. Place two chicken parts on this, cover with another layer of leaves, add the next two parts and cover with the remaining leaves. Add meat stock to the pot until the meat is just covered, add mace, and bring to a boil. Simmer at low heat for 20–30 minutes. Add butter to the pot before serving.

Arrange each portion of meat on a mound of lettuce leaves. Serve hot with bread.

This recipe also works with a whole chicken quartered for serving portions, but it needs to be cooked longer. Most days, Landsknechts probably enjoyed old hens with cabbage or beet greens rather than lettuce.

Steamed Capon

This is a highly extravagant luxury dish that could have been improvised by an officer's cook in camp. The required pewter pitchers were popular with Landsknechts, and the ingredients could be acquired in any larger city with money (or threats of violence). *Malvasier* (Malmsey) and *Reinfal* (Ribolla gialla) were the most expensive wines, and the spices further signalled wealth. We can simulate the cooking technique in a closed canning jar today.

To make steamed capons

Take a good capon or more and stick it well about with cloves, mace, nutmeg, cinnamon, ginger, and not much salt. Then take a pewter pitcher that the capon fits into, cover it well so that no steam can escape it and pour a measure of Malvasier *or* Reinfal *with the capon. Set the pitcher with the capon into a cauldron with boiling water, let it boil in there for three or four hours, and close it up well so that no water can get in. Seal the lid with paste and wrap a linen cloth around it. Thus you will have a good dish.*

(Sabina Welser, #1)

2½ HOURS

INGREDIENTS

SERVES 4

- 1 cinnamon stick
- 1 whole nutmeg
- 5 cm / 2 inches of dried ginger
- 4 chicken legs
- Whole mace leaves
- Whole cloves
- Salt
- 1 L / 4 cups white Malvasia or another strong white wine

The chicken legs are cooked in two 1-litre canning jars.

Cut the cinnamon stick into long slivers. Carefully cut the nutmeg and ginger into long, pointy slices. Wash and pat dry the chicken legs and pierce them all over with a small, pointy knife. Alternately fill the incisions with a clove, a piece of nutmeg, ginger, cinnamon, or a piece of mace. Place two legs in each jar and lightly salt them. Divide the wine between the jars and close them well.

Boil the jars immersed in a large pot of water for 90 minutes. Alternatively, stand them in a deep baking dish, fill up with water to a depth of 1–2 cm, and bake in a 200°C / 400°F oven for 2 hours.

Serve with fine white bread accompanied by wine.

Broiled Fish

Fresh fish was a luxury food and generally most likely limited to officers. Artfully arranged, it adorned feasting tables. Broiling was a simpler preparation, and the cookbook of Philippine Welser records the method in detail. Should a fish ever have found its way to the cookfire of a *Rotte* of Landsknecht soldiers, it could have been prepared this way. Imported spices, of course, would be used less lavishly.

If you would make good broiled fish
Take the fish and cut it open and salt it. Then add good vinegar and let it lie in that for half an hour. Afterwards, take marjoram, rosemary, sage, or what other good herbs you have together. Also take three walnuts and a few juniper berries. Pound all of that in a mortar. Take pepper and ginger powder, stir all of that together, and fill it into the fish. Stick it on a wooden skewer, lay it on a griddle, and let it broil nicely cool. Take vinegar in a small pan, add a little oil or butter, some juniper berries and pepper, and saffron. Let it boil together and brush the fish with this as often as you turn it until it is done.

(Philippine Welser, p. 105 r)

INGREDIENTS

SERVES 2

1 HOUR

2 trout (or other whole freshwater fish)
Salt
250 ml / 1 cup vinegar
6 walnut kernels
Fresh herbs as desired
Juniper berries
Pepper
Ginger
50 g / 5 tablespoons butter
or 50 ml / 4 tablespoons oil
Saffron if desired

Preheat the oven to 175°C / 350°F. Wash and salt the fish and lay out in a shallow bowl. Cover with 150 ml vinegar and leave for 30 minutes. Meanwhile, finely chop the walnuts, herbs, and a few juniper berries. Season the filling with pepper and ginger and divide it between the fish. Place both fish in an open baking dish. Heat the remaining vinegar in a saucepan with the butter or oil, some crushed juniper berries, pepper, and saffron if desired. Brush the fish with the mixture and cook in the oven for 25 minutes, brushing again regularly. Serve hot.

STOCKFISH

Stockfish

Stockfish, dried cod imported from Norway, was one of the few kinds of fish affordable to most people as an everyday food. Despite a large number of surviving recipes, it does not seem to have been popular. It was eaten on fast days for want of other options. A commonplace method of cooking it is found in Staindl:

Boil a piece of stockfish as long as you boil a proper fish, take it, lay it in cold water, and pick out the bones and all uncleanness. Place it in a pot, cut onions, fry them in fat, and put that in with the fish. Let it boil as long as a proper fish, colour it yellow, season it and add some raisins. Serve it on toasted bread.

(Staindl, #129)

3 DAYS PRE-SOAKING, 45 MINUTES COOKING

INGREDIENTS

SERVES 4

- 500-750 g / 1-1½ lbs stockfish
- Water
- 2-3 onions
- 2 tablespoons lard or butter
- Saffron
- 100 g / 4 oz raisins
- Spices as desired
  (e.g., ginger, pepper, and mace)

The size of the piece of stockfish required can vary greatly, depending on how much of it consists of skin and bones.

The stockfish needs to be soaked in fresh water prior to cooking for at least 72 hours. Change the water at least once daily. The fish is ready to cook when it is no longer hard, but still firm.

Simmer the soaked stockfish in fresh water. Remove after 10–15 minutes and chill. Reserve the cooking water. Carefully flake the fish with bare fingers, removing all skin and bones.

Finely dice the onions and sauté them in the lard or butter in a saucepan until they begin browning. Add the flaked fish and a little of the cooking water. Dissolve the saffron, if desired, and add the raisins. Simmer for 10–15 minutes, then salt and season to taste. Serve hot on toasted bread.

This recipe is plausible as an inexpensive dish if the spices and raisins are omitted.

Bread Pudding Cooked in a Stomach

The recipe collection of Meister Hans contains a description of how a prince's cooks turn a single calf into a multitude of dishes. This also includes a preparation of bread cooked in a stomach that looks like a modern *Serviettenknödel*. It would certainly not have been beyond the capabilities of a *Sudler* to prepare. In the modern kitchen, a pudding cloth is substituted.

And he takes bacon and white wheat bread, he cuts it into cubes. Take eggs as many as you wish and the bacon and bread with it, and fill the stomach and gullet, let it boil nicely, and boil it separately.

(Meister Hans, #190)

1½ HOURS

INGREDIENTS

SIDE DISH FOR 4

100 g / 4 oz bacon
250 g / 4 cups dry cubed white bread
4 eggs
Salt
Butter
Flour

Dice the bacon. Knead the bread cubes in a bowl with the bacon and the eggs and salt to taste. Lay out a pudding cloth or a clean, undamaged dish towel on a work surface, spread it with butter and dust it with flour. Place the bread mass on it, shape roughly into a sausage, and roll up. Tie both ends tightly with string.

Carefully lower into a large pot of boiling water and simmer for 60 minutes. Remove with two slotted spoons, drain off excess water, open the strings with scissors and carefully unroll. Slice and serve hot.

Green Tart of Chard

Tarts and pastries of all kinds were popular in the sixteenth century, and one recipe we keep encountering in many sources is a "green tart" made with various herbs, cheese, and eggs. Not overly complex, but rich and fashionably Italian, the appeal is easy to see. The recipe can be varied according to taste and availability of ingredients, but it is fairly clear it is meant to be prepared with hard, aged cheese, quite possibly Parmesan imported from Italy at great cost. Recipes sometimes specify the herbs involved, but these vary so much it is clear what was wanted was colour and texture rather than a specific flavour. The example quoted here is one of the earliest recorded German ones, from the fifteenth-century Innsbruck manuscript:

If you want to make a tart, take chard, salt, and parsley, chop it up small, and wash it in fresh water. Grate cheese into it, add fat and eggs, and then make sheets of dough and fill it into them. Bake it in a (baking) pan, put egg yolk on top, and leave it to bake well etc.

(Innsbruck MS, #146)

INGREDIENTS

SERVES 4

60-75 MINUTES

- 1 head of Swiss chard (or 500 g / 1 lb spinach)
- 1 bunch parsley
- 150 g / 5 oz grated cheese (e.g., Parmesan, aged Gouda, or Emmental)
- 4 eggs
- Salt
- Pepper
- Nutmeg
- 50 g / 5 tablespoons butter
- Pastry crust

Wash the chard and remove the hard stems from the leaves (if using frozen spinach, thaw). Finely chop the leaves together with the parsley. If they are very tough, parboiling them may be a good idea. Mix them with the beaten eggs and the grated cheese and season to taste with salt, pepper, and nutmeg or other spices and herbs. Fill into a pastry crust, dot with butter and bake at 180°C / 350°F for 35–45 minutes, until a knife inserted in the centre comes out clean.

A number of different recipes for pastry crust survive from Renaissance German sources, but for our purposes, storebought is fine.

Grünkern Porridge

Grünkern is spelt harvested unripe and dried, a product similar to *freekeh* that is still widely sold in Germany today. The technique is described in the *Kuchenmaistrey*. Especially in mountainous regions where the grain did not always fully ripen before the rains set in, this could be lifesaving for poor farmers. Peasants stored such dried grain in sheaves, and Landsknechts in quarter surely helped themselves to it. The recipe mentions several added ingredients that would have suited them well if they could get them. Bacon, at least, was part of the stores in any properly run household.

To keep ears of corn over the year, whether spelt or wheat, take them green, i.e. when they are fresh, and dry them in an oven or in the sun. Store them high, like cherries. When you wish to have them, lay them in fresh well water and they will return to their virtue. Boil them with young chickens or prepare them with small pieces of bacon and salt or with butter. Gamebirds boiled with it, too, are good and easily digested. You can also keep dried pears this way.

(*Kuchenmaistrey*, I. XLIII)

30–45 MINUTES

INGREDIENTS

SIDE DISH FOR 4

100 g / 4 oz bacon

250 g / ½ lb *Grünkern* or *freekeh*, coarsely ground

600 ml / 2 ½ cups meat stock (or salted water)

1 tablespoon butter

Dice the bacon and heat it in a pot or cast-iron skillet. Quickly sauté the *Grünkern* or *freekeh* in it, then add the meat stock. Boil it up once, then simmer for 5 minutes, stirring occasionally. Close the lid and finish cooking at the lowest setting until soft. This takes about 20 minutes. Melt the butter on the finished porridge and stir in.

If only one pot is available, any greens can be cooked in the porridge. If you wish to add larger pieces of meat such as entire chickens, more cooking liquid is needed and the cooking time is extended according to their size. Drain excess liquid at the end.

Lentils

Legumes were a staple on poor people's tables, but we rarely find instructions how to cook them. Balthasar Staindl records a lentil recipe that could be used as a meal in its own right, but also served as a side dish.

Slowly boil the lentils, add fried onions to them, sour them, season them, add raisins and serve them on toasted bread as a supper dish.

(Staindl, #257)

INGREDIENTS

SIDE DISH FOR 4

30 MINUTES

- 200 g / 7 oz lentils
- Water
- 1 onion
- 1 teaspoon lard or butter
- Salt
- Vinegar
- Spices as desired (e.g., nutmeg and pepper)
- 50 g / 2 oz raisins

Soak the lentils in plenty of cold water overnight. Drain and put them in a pot with twice the amount of fresh water by volume and simmer for 20 minutes, stirring occasionally. Meanwhile dice the onion and sauté it in the lard or butter until browned. When the lentils are soft, stir in the onion. Season to taste with salt, vinegar, and spices if desired. Strew with raisins and serve hot on toast.

A simpler version without spices or raisins can be eaten like a soup with bread.

Pea Porridge

Pea porridge was a popular side dish accompanying both fish and meat and could be a meal by itself. It was produced from dried peas cooked in water or broth. The simplest method was to cook shelled peas in a pot until they disintegrated when stirred. By carefully pouring off excess cooking liquid, a firm purée could be produced. The remaining pea broth was used for cooking on fast days. Balthasar Staindl's detailed recipe is for meat days:

Take peas that are nicely white in a lye. Rub them between your hands, then they will release their shells. Wash them and dry them again. When you wish to make pea porridge, set a piece of pork to cook, pour the same broth with the same peas and let them boil soft that way. Pass them through a cloth, or if you have a lot, you can grind them in a mill so they turn out thick and mix them with pork broth to a thickness as if you wanted to cook porridge. Boil them in a clean pot. When you serve it, cut good bacon in small cubes, sauté it a little and strew it over the pea porridge. Place a slice of bread in the middle and put the pork on it. Sometimes, you also pour a little cream into it.

(Staindl, #277)

24 HOURS SOAKING, 90 MINUTES COOKING

INGREDIENTS

SERVES 4

400 g / 1 lb split peas
Water
2 L / 8 cups meat stock
200 g / 7 oz bacon
Salt

Soak the peas in water overnight. Drain and simmer in meat stock for 60–90 minutes until soft. Dice and sauté the bacon.

When the peas are soft, but do not yet fall apart on their own, carefully drain the broth and mash or purée them. Add a little of the broth to achieve the consistency of porridge and salt to taste. Add bacon and serve hot.

Pea porridge goes well with boiled meat (see p. 72), but it can also be served with herring or gamebirds.

Kraut

The smell of boiled cabbage carried the stigma of poverty well into modernity. It was the food of the common peasants and townsfolk, rarely mentioned in recipes, but ubiquitous. Those who looked to their status chose different types of greens, such as spinach or chard, that are mentioned in cookbooks with greater frequency. The *Kuchenmaistrey* gives instructions how to avoid the scent of destitution:

Of leafy greens that are commonly eaten such as chard, spinach and Compost *(pickled cabbage), you should clean them well, lay them in the pot and boil them. Always pour off the water thoroughly when they are half cooked. And the water that you pour in in its place should be well salted and be cooked until done. And if you wish to make broth, it is good to chop the leaves, but the cooking water is too strong and foul-smelling, that is why you must take away the water, be they chopped or whole.*

(*Kuchenmaistrey*, 4. XXV)

UP TO 1½ HOURS

INGREDIENTS

SIDE DISH FOR 4

750 g / 1½ lbs fresh spinach or chard (for upscale cooking)

or 1 small head of cabbage

Water

Salt or meat stock

Lard or butter

Separate the leaves, wash them thoroughly and chop them coarsely. Remove the thickest parts of the base from cabbage leaves. Simmer till soft in plenty of lightly salted water. Spinach wilts in minutes while cabbage can take an hour or more without a pressure cooker. Pour off the cooking water, fill up with meat stock or fresh salted water and return to a boil. Serve hot, dabbed with butter or lard.

Plain cabbage, *Kraut,* was buttered and served with bread. On richer tables, it served as a side dish with meat or fish. *Sudler* cooks, too, probably served it with each portion of boiled meat.

Rüben

Cabbage and root vegetables—the proverbial *Kraut und Rüben*—were the daily fare of the poor. Every farmhouse kept a store, and many townsfolk had small gardens outside the walls to grow their own. They were boiled and eaten with bread like a soup. The state of the purse determined what further ingredients there were, if any.

Little is said about these dishes in cookbooks. They were both too humble and too varied. *Rüben* could refer to all kinds of root vegetable. The *Kuchenmaistrey* holds instructions for dealing with dried root vegetables, a food for the lean springtime months. Smoked pork from last year's slaughter remained a fond dream for many.

Of dried Rüben *and turnips it is best to boil them with the smoked meat of young pigs and season them with butter and salt. That is proper.*

(*Kuchenmaistrey*, 1. XLIIII)

UP TO 1 HOUR

INGREDIENTS

SERVES 4

750 g / 1½ lbs root vegetables
100 g / 4 oz smoked bacon
1 tablespoon butter
Water (or meat stock)
Salt

Parsnips, turnips, beets, and carrots are all suitable for this, though today's sweet orange carrots are a relatively modern development.

Wash, peel, and cut the roots into bite-sized pieces. Dice the bacon. Briefly sauté the root vegetables in the bottom of a pot and fill up with water or meat stock until just covered. Simmer until soft. Depending on the type of root, this can take between 20 and 45 minutes. Salt to taste.

In lean times, there would be no bacon or butter, at best some fat from the mixed pot (see p. 39). When there was more money or a well-appointed household to loot, the quantity of meat increased accordingly.

Leeks in Milk

Leeks were eaten frequently, and we have several recipes combining them with almond milk. One late medieval recipe collection from Munich includes a similar recipe using plain milk which very likely was by far more common.

Take leeks, greens, and cabbage. Cut them the length of a digit and sauté them in fat. Add water and bring it to a boil. Place it in a sieve, the water drains off. Then lay it in a pot and pour in milk that was passed through a cloth with white bread, and add fat.

(Staatsbibliothek München 384 I, #14)

INGREDIENTS

SIDE DISH FOR 4

45 MINUTES

- 50 g dry white bread or breadcrumbs / ¾ cup if cubed bread, ½ cup if breadcrumbs
- 500 ml / 2 cups milk
- 1 kg / 2 lbs leeks (mixed with greens if desired)
- Butter
- Water
- Salt

Soak the bread in the milk and purée. Wash the leeks, remove the green parts and slice the white part into 2 cm rounds. Melt a dab of butter in a pot, briefly sauté the leeks and fill up with lightly salted water until just covered. Simmer for 10 minutes, then pour off the water and add the milk. Simmer for a further 15–20 minutes, stirring regularly. The leeks fall apart and the milk reduces to a creamy consistency. Salt to taste.

This goes very well with chicken or pork.

Mus of Apples or Pears

Foreign visitors often remarked how commonly fruit was used in German cooking. Apples or pears were cooked into a side dish that goes well with pork, and recipes are frequently found in cookbooks.

A Mus *of pears: Take a wide, flat pot, cut pears into it that are good, peel onions, and add wine, salt, and fat. Cover it well and set it in the embers, it softens and mushes itself. Serve it and strew it with ginger.*

(*Kuchenmaistrey*, 1. XLVIII)

An apple Mus *with onions make thus as well: Cut small slices, a little milk or wine, also spices, salt and fat. Cover it well and let it simmer on a small fire.*

(*Kuchenmaistrey*, 1. XLIX)

Apples and pears were not just eaten fresh in season, but also dried. Marx Rumpolt gives a recipe for dried apples:

Dried apples are boiled in clear water, especially by the common man in the villages for he does not have as much gear as a great lord. He must make do with what he has.

(Rumpolt, p. CXLIIII r)

APPLE (OR PEAR) MUS

INGREDIENTS

SIDE DISH FOR 4

500 g / 1 lb aromatic tart apples (or cooking pears)
2 mild onions
Lard or butter
125 ml / ½ cup dry white wine (or milk or water)
Salt
Spices as desired

45 MINUTES

Peel, core, and coarsely cut the apples. Slice the onions into thin rings. Melt the lard or butter in a pot and sauté the onions. Add the wine and the apples and simmer with a closed lid until the apple pieces fall apart. Stir and salt and season to taste (e.g., with cinnamon, cloves, and pepper).

MUS OF DRIED APPLES

INGREDIENTS

SIDE DISH FOR 4

200 g / 3 ½ cups dried apple chips
Water
Salt

24 HOURS SOAKING, 30 MINUTES COOKING

Soak the apple chips in water overnight. Drain, place in a pot, and barely cover with some of the soaking water. Simmer gently, stirring regularly, and add more of the soaking water as needed. The dish is finished once the apples fall apart.

Storable Sauces

Sauces were part of fine cooking. Poor people made do with vinegar. We can assume that most surviving sauce recipes were not widespread among Landsknechts. However, our sources include a number of recipes intended for long storage and even for travel. We can easily see those in the baggage of an officer's cook or even for sale in camp markets.

SAUCE OF TART CHERRIES

If you would make a good sauce of tart cherries, place them in a pot and set them in the embers. Let them boil up and cool again, then pass them through a cloth. Set them in the embers again and let them boil well. Stir them until they thicken, then add honey, grated bread, cloves, and good spices. Put the sauce into a small vat. It stays good for three or four years.

(Meister Eberhard, #1)

The sauce tastes best made from fresh tart cherries, but it can also be made with frozen or canned ones. If you are using sweetened canned cherries, it takes less honey. It is easier to pit the cherries before cooking them instead of removing them by passing them though a cloth.

INGREDIENTS

FOR STORAGE

300-400 g / 10-14 oz tart cherries, pitted

Honey

Cloves

Pepper, cinnamon, ginger and other spices as desired

2-3 tablespoons breadcrumbs

20 MINUTES

Purée the pitted cherries and bring them to a boil in a saucepan. Sweeten to taste with honey and season with cloves and other spices as desired. Simmer at low heat for about 10–15 minutes, then gradually stir in the breadcrumbs until it dissolves and thickens.

This sauce can be filled hot into sterilised jars and stored like jam. It will keep for months.

GARLIC SAUCE

For garlic sauce, you need a little sifted breadcrumbs soaked in vinegar. (It is) pounded well with lean meat broth and seasoned with salt and a little vinegar. Keep the sauce in a well-stoppered bottle, that way it retains its virtue.

(*Kuchenmaistrey*, 4. IIII)

This garlic sauce is easy to produce and store.

INGREDIENTS

FOR STORAGE

2 bulbs of garlic
250 ml / 1 cup meat stock
4–6 tablespoons breadcrumbs
Salt
Vinegar

15 MINUTES

Peel and coarsely chop garlic. Add hot meat stock and purée. Once the liquid is smooth, gradually add the breadcrumbs and keep processing until the sauce thickens. Add salt and vinegar to taste.

Like the cherry sauce, this sauce can be kept in jars, though it tastes best fresh. If a clear liquid separates out during storage, just shake the jar.

GREEN SAUCE FROM DRIED HERBS

Make a green sauce thus, and keep it
Take sage with onions, parsley, and old and young sorrel. Pick the herbs, wash them, and dry them in the sun. Also take pepper, galingale, ginger, cinnamon, anise, coriander, cubeb pepper, cloves, mace, grains of paradise, and a little Artickel (?), *that makes the sage nice. Then take dried white bread and grind everything to a powder. When you wish to eat it, mix it with wine or vinegar, and keep this as long as you want.*

(Meister Hans, #81)

We do not know what exactly *Artickel* is, but this is no problem for a plausible reconstruction. Several similar recipes use varying mixes of herbs and spices. None give quantities, leaving great leeway for interpretation. I have had good success with this mix:

INGREDIENTS

SIDE DISH FOR 4

30-45 MINUTES PREPARATION, 2 MINUTES MIXING

- 6 peppercorns
- ¼ teaspoon galingale
- ¼ teaspoon ginger
- 1 pinch of cinnamon
- 1 pinch of anise
- 1 pinch of coriander
- 3 cloves
- 4 cubeb pepper corns
- 10 grains of paradise
- 1 leaf of mace
- 3 teaspoons dried parsley
- 3 teaspoons dried sage
- 2 teaspoons dried sorrel
- 2 teaspoons dried onions
- 2 tablespoons breadcrumbs

First, grind the spices to a powder in a mortar or mill. Next, grind the dried herbs in a mortar or turn them into a powder in a food processor at high speed. Finally, combine both with the breadcrumbs and grind of process into a fine, homogeneous powder. This takes considerable patience to do in a mortar.

Kept dry, the finished powder can be stored for a long time. To mix it, gradually stir in vinegar until a thick liquid results. Salt is not mentioned in the recipe, but it works well in the mix. This green sauce harmonises well with chicken or pork.

ZISEINDEL (APPLE SAUCE)

Ziseindel

We meet a savoury sauce of apples, with or without onions, in cookbooks over more than a century. It often goes by the name of *Ziseindel* or *Preseindel*. Served with meat or fish, it seems to have been universally popular. *Ziseindel* cannot be preserved and thus was only available while apples could be had, usually from late summer until the following spring. Balthasar Staindl describes its preparation with the superficiality of a bored professional:

If you would make a chopped sauce, chop apples, sauté them, and do as is described above. You also make it with onions. At times, you also take apples and onions together. You serve this over venison, cakes, or whatever you wish to serve with this sauce.

(Staindl, #46)

30-45 MINUTES

INGREDIENTS

SIDE DISH FOR 4

3 tart aromatic apples
2 mild onions
1 tablespoon lard or butter
Vinegar
Sugar or honey
Spices as desired

Peel, core, and dice the apples. Finely chop the onions. Melt the fat in a saucepan and sauté the onions. Add a dash of vinegar, simmer until soft, then add the apples and continue cooking until they fall apart. If necessary, add water by the tablespoon to prevent burning. Sweeten with a little sugar or honey and add spices as desired. Sabina Welser recommends cinnamon, ginger and saffron.

A sauce made with onions only needs more liquid and stronger spices such as pepper and nutmeg.

Berry Sauces

Sauces made with berries were especially popular with meat, a fact foreigners often remarked on with wonder. They were a seasonal delicacy, available only for a brief time in summer when berries could be gathered. The Innsbruck manuscript holds two brief recipes:

COWBERRY SAUCE

If you would make a sauce of cowberries, take grated gingerbread (Lebkuchen) *and pass it through a cloth with wine or with vinegar. Pound the berries beforehand etc.*

(Innsbruck MS, #116)

10 MINUTES

INGREDIENTS

SIDE DISH FOR 4

2 tablespoons ground dry gingerbread
50 ml / 4 tablespoons wine
200 g / 7 oz fresh cowberries (or cranberries)

Soak the gingerbread in the wine. Purée the cowberries and mix with the soaked gingerbread.

For modern tastes, some sweetener is usually called for. This sauce goes well with beef roast or venison.

RASPBERRY SAUCE

A sauce of raspberries: Pound them, pass them through a cloth with wine and season them so that they are sweet, or also add honey etc.

(Innsbruck MS, #123)

INGREDIENTS

SIDE DISH FOR 4

5 MINUTES

250 g / ½ lb raspberries
2–3 tablespoons white wine
Honey

Purée the raspberries and add wine and honey to taste. This sauce works well with roast chickens or ducks, but also with cheese fritters.

Mustard

Mustard was an inexpensive, readily available, and popular condiment. The simplest preparation is not detailed anywhere and only briefly mentioned by Marx Rumpolt:

Brown mustard made with clear vinegar is also good.

(Rumpolt, p. CLX r)

This was the mustard that Landsknechts were familiar with and that they likely could buy in camp markets sometimes. Mustard pots belonged in every properly stocked pantry. However, many recipe books also include a sweet honey mustard with various spices. One late fifteenth-century manuscript even includes an instant version:

For a good mustard, take mustard seed, dry it cleanly and grind it very finely in a mortar. Then pass it through a fine cloth. Take cinnamon flower and mix it with the mustard, and then stir it with honey so that it becomes (firm) like wax. And if you wish to eat of it, take a little of the same and grind it with wine, then you have good mustard.

(Staatsbibliothek München Cgm 384 I, #12)

Sabina Welser also includes a recipe for a mustard made with pear electuary to be served with stockfish. There were few limits to luxury.

10 MINUTES PREPARATION, 2 MINUTES MIXING

INGREDIENTS

FOR STORAGE

100 g / ⅓ cup firm honey
50 g / ⅓ cup mustard flour
Ground cinnamon flower buds or cinnamon
White wine

Warm the honey in a double boiler until it liquefies. Stir in the mustard flour and season with cinnamon flower to taste. If cinnamon flower is not available, plain cinnamon will do as well. Pour into a glass jar and cool.

To serve, mix one tablespoon of the mixture with a little white wine in a small bowl until a thick liquid results. Let the mustard stand for some time before serving. It is very potent by modern standards.

Triget

Many apothecaries and grocers sold ready-made spice mixes that could ease the life of inexperienced cooks and were sometimes carried by travellers to make unprepossessing food palatable. The latter surely was no habit of common soldiers, but these mixes were a comparatively affordable luxury and probably not uncommon among officers at least.

Triget, a sweet spice mixture often used on egg dishes and porridge, is frequently mentioned. Balthasar Staindl records a recipe.

Take two Lot *of white ginger, four* Lot *of cinnamon quills of the long kind, and half a* Lot *of mace. Make that into a powder. Take as much sugar as you have spices, but if you do not want to have it sweet, takes less sugar, or if you want it very sweet, take more. This is good with toasted bread slices.*

(Staindl, #247)

We cannot say for sure which *Lot* is used here. Measures could differ considerably between cities. The proportions are clear, though. For a small store, we get:

INGREDIENTS

FOR STORAGE

5 MINUTES

20 g / 0.7 oz ground cinnamon
10 g / 0.35 oz ground ginger
3 g / 0.1 oz ground mace
30 g / 1 oz fine sugar

Mix the spices and sugar. If you want to grind them fresh, you need to add a little sugar to the mortar with the mace to prevent it from oiling. Carried in a wooden box or leather bag, Triget could serve a traveller well.

Electuary of Quinces

Electuaries were a popular, though very expensive way of preserving fruit with sugar. Originally medicinal, the word means "something to be licked": a thick, sweet paste. Several recipes mention them as ingredients in sauces, and they were eaten as sweets. For a common Landsknecht, they would have been a rare luxury, but they were not strangers to conspicuous luxury in good times. Marx Rumpolt's recipe is for quinces, but electuaries were also made with apples or pears.

Take quinces and grate them, put them into a sack and squeeze them. Place (the juice) in a clean vessel, set it on the coals and let it boil. Add the quinces that you sliced small and fine into the juice and let it boil together. Take a clean wooden spoon and mash the quinces until they become thick. When it has boiled down well, add white sugar that has been clarified and let it boil until it thickens. Place it in a clean box. This is how you make a chunky electuary.

(Rumpolt, p. CLXXXII r)

3-4 HOURS

INGREDIENTS

FOR STORAGE

2 kg / 4 lbs quinces
1 kg / 2 lbs sugar

Making the juice: Wash half the quinces and rub off the fuzz from the skin. Cut into chunks and simmer in a wide pot barely covered with water until very soft. Strain off the cooking liquid, then wrap the solids in a clean dish towel and press out the remaining juice. Reserve.

Cooking the electuary: Wash, peel, and core the other half of the quinces, making sure to remove all woody parts. Slice thinly and simmer with the juice, stirring continually. When the slices begin to fall apart, add the sugar and keep stirring as the mass cooks. It is ready to be put in jars when the bottom of the pot remains visible for a few moments during stirring. This can take an hour or more of patient cooking. Fill into jars or bowls hot and allow to set.

Spiced Vinegar

Vinegar was the most common condiment, used by even the poorest. The word *Essig* did not distinguish between vinegar, alegar, fruit vinegar, verjuice, and other similar condiments. If it was sour, it was *Essig*. People were well aware of gradations in quality, though. The kind of vinegar sixteenth-century cooks wanted was roughly what we can buy as high-end wine vinegar today. Apple vinegar, too, was popular in some areas. Neither 'white' spirit vinegar nor the sweet balsamico varieties were known.

Some vinegars were infused with spices and herbs for medicinal and culinary use. Hieronymus Bock records a recipe:

Temper with it all manner of spices such as grains of paradise, ginger, pepper, and pellitory root. Let it stand for a while in a vessel that is not too full. Then you have good alegar.

(Bock, p. LV v)

Few of us will feel like brewing our own vinegar, but spice infusions can be made with the store-bought kind. These sauces were more suited for an officer's table, though.

INGREDIENTS

FOR STORAGE

10 MINUTES

- 2 cm / 1 inch dried ginger root
- 20 peppercorns
- 40 grains of paradise
- 1 tablespoon chopped dried pellitory root
- 750 ml / 3 cups vinegar or alegar

Coarsely chop the ginger root. Place all spices and the vinegar in a bottle, close, and let stand in a cool, dark place for 4 weeks.

Strauben

The simplest kind of the ever-popular fritters were known as *Strauben*. They were so familiar that the consistency of their batter is used as a reference in many recipes. Balthasar Staindl is one of the few authors to describe how they are made:

Take good flour and then take yeast that comes from beer and pour as much into the flour as an egg. Then take lukewarm water and make a batter, salt it, and make it as thick as the starter you make for baking bread. Rest it so that it rises. When you wish to fry them, take lukewarm water, wet your hands, take a little dough into your hands, pull it apart and fry it well in hot fat. You can also fry them in oil.

(Staindl, #215)

Strauben batter could also be enriched with eggs or milk. Pulled into strips and fried crisp, this familiar treat came in many varieties.

1½ HOURS

INGREDIENTS

SERVES 4

- ½ cube of fresh yeast (or 1 teaspoon active dry yeast)
- 125–150 ml / ½ cup water
- 1 pinch of salt
- 250 g / 1¾ cups all-purpose flour
- Fat or oil for frying

Dissolve the yeast in the water and let rest for 15 minutes. Then work it into a dough with the flour and a pinch of salt. Add more water as necessary. The batter should be sticky, but not runny. Cover and let rise in a warm place for 45 minutes.

To fry, pick up a ping-pong-ball sized piece of the matter with wet fingers, quickly pull into a string and immediately drop into the hot fat. The *Strauben* are ready to serve in 5–7 minutes. They can accompany sweet or savoury dishes.

CROOKED FRITTERS

Crooked Fritters

Cheese fritters, rich and filling, occur in many variations across surviving cookbooks. The combination was popular and we know that street vendors sold a specific type in Nuremberg during carnival. The *Kuchenmaistrey* has a recipe in which the cheese dough is cut into strips and served in a sauce. Sabina Welser describes parmesan worked into balls with eggs and flour and fried in a dough crust. The *Inntalkochbuch* keeps it simple:

For fritters as crooked as horseshoes
Grate good cheese and take with it half as much flour and break eggs into it so you can knead it, and spices. Roll it out on a bench so that it becomes like a sausage. Then make it crooked and fry it in fat.

(*Inntalkochbuch*, #5)

30 MINUTES

INGREDIENTS

SERVES 4

- 250 g / ½ lb grated cheese
- 125 g / ¾ cup all-purpose flour
- 2-3 eggs
- Spices as desired
- Fat for frying

Firm, aromatic cheeses like Emmental or Cheddar are well suited to this recipe, but a milder version can also be made with a young Gouda. Very hard, dry cheeses like parmesan or pecorino may require more egg to bind them. Choose spices to match the cheese; pepper and mace with aromatic types, cloves, ginger, and nutmeg with milder ones. Salt should be used with great care if at all.

Work cheese, flour, eggs, and spices into a firm dough. Roll into 1 cm thick, finger-length strings with floured hands and bend into horseshoe shapes. Fry crisp and serve hot.

Crooked fritters can easily be fried in a pan with a smaller amount of fat if you turn them over regularly. They can also be baked in an oven for an even lower-fat version, but that is contrary to the spirit of the thing.

Krapfen

Krapfen referred to all kinds of filled dough dumplings. Most were fried. Fillings could vary widely, and several recipes for different doughs survive. Various sources mention honey and wine, beer, eggs, or plain water paste. Marx Rumpolt uses the same rich yeast dough also used for a cake and suggests cherry sauce (see p. 119) as a filling:

Make a dough with milk, eggs, and fine white flour. Add a little beer yeast to it and make a good dough that is not too stiff, and do not oversalt it. Set it in a warm place so that it rises well. [...]

Take such a dough and roll it out. Wrap cherry sauce in it, cut it off with a pastry wheel, throw it on butter, fry it, and serve it warm. Strew it with white sugar, thus they are good Krapfen *of cherry sauce. You can make such* Krapfen *of all kinds of sauce.*

(Rumpolt, p. CLXVIII v)

KRAPFEN DOUGH

2 HOURS

INGREDIENTS

SERVES 4

- 1 cube of fresh yeast (or 2 teaspoons active dry yeast)
- 150 ml / ½–⅔ cup milk
- 350 g / 2 ¾ cups all-purpose or pastry flour
- 2 eggs
- Extra flour to work the dough

Dissolve the yeast in the lukewarm milk and leave to develop for 10 minutes. Work into an elastic dough with the flour and eggs. Knead well, cover, and leave to rise in a warm place for 45 minutes.

Roll out the dough on a floured work surface and cut in any shape you wish. Most *Krapfen* were likely square or circular, but Anna Wecker also describes artistically decorated animal and flower shapes. Place one spoonful of filling in the centre of each *Krapfen*. Wet the edges with water or beaten egg. Fold over and press shut carefully. Allow them to rise again for 10 minutes on a floured surface, taking care that the dough does not stick, otherwise it will tear open on lifting them. Fry in hot fat for 5–7 minutes.

Leavened *Krapfen* can also be baked in an oven, and this was done at the time. Brush them with beaten egg yolk and bake at 180°C / 350°F for 20 minutes.

You could basically put anything you wanted into *Krapfen*. Fruit fillings were very popular, not just the much-loved cherry sauce, but also one made with apples:

APPLE FILLING

Take Italian raisins and take many apples with them and pound them small. Add spices and fill that into the Krapfen, *let them fry, and do not oversalt it.*
(*Mondseer Kochbuch*, #55)

INGREDIENTS

2–3 tart aromatic apples
100 g / 4 oz raisins
Spices as desired (e.g., cinnamon, ginger, cloves)
Honey or sugar if desired

15 MINUTES

Peel, core, and finely dice the apples. Mix with the raisins, knead thoroughly, and season to taste. The filling can be further sweetened if desired, but for contemporaries adding raisins would have been sweetener enough.

HERB FILLING

Savoury herb fillings were also popular. They were bound with egg and sometimes cheese. The exact composition was left to the discretion of the cook and probably varied with the seasons and availability of ingredients.

If you would make Krapfen *of eggs, you can chop parsley or dropwort and other good herbs, add them and knead them with raw egg, season them, salt them, and fill them.*

(*Kuchenmaistrey*, 3. XIII)

INGREDIENTS

1 bunch parsley

Herbs as desired (e.g., thyme, marjoram, sage, sorrel or lovage)

3-4 eggs

Salt

Pepper or other spices if desired

Cheese or cottage cheese if desired

10 MINUTES

Wash, dry, and finely chop all herbs, but do not purée them. Mix with the beaten eggs. Salt and season to taste. This filling can be further enriched with grated cheese or cottage cheese. *Krapfen* of this kind must be fried thoroughly so the egg cooks all the way through.

MEAT FILLING

Meat was also used to fill *Krapfen*, especially when leftovers could be used up this way. The instructions given in the *Kuchenmaistrey* are slightly confusing, but the basic idea is to combine meat, eggs, and herbs. It is important to remember that the meat must indeed be cooked beforehand. *Krapfen* are not fried long enough to fully cook a raw meat filling.

[...] But what you wish to fill with meat, any meat filling or fish filling must be properly and well cooked beforehand. Be it gamebird or spleen, lungs, liver, or whatever other small meats, it must be chopped well and pounded in a mortar well. What you add of eggs, of pears, or calf's head, you must add parsley and other aromatic herbs of the kind you use a little of for fillings, for flavour's sake. [...] and also when you make the filling for chickens or pigeons or whatever other meat there is, you need the good herbs and also juniper berries ground together with caraway and fennel. Mix that with the filling together with raw eggs, kneaded well together, filled in and fried well.

(*Kuchenmaistrey*, 3. XIIII)

INGREDIENTS

10 MINUTES

200-300 g / 7-10 oz cooked meat
2-3 eggs
Herbs and spices as desired

Cube the meat, then process it into a paste with the eggs and herbs. Salt and season to taste (chicken goes well with the fennel seed and caraway suggested here). Wrap in *Krapfen* dough and fry.

Waffles

Fresh, hot waffles have been popular market fare for a long time. Pieter Breughel's famous *Battle of Carnival and Lent* already shows a woman baking them in the open air. A bowl of batter, a waffle iron, and a small fire were enough to keep her in business. The setup in army camp markets must have looked very similar.

A simple waffle recipe is found in the cookbook of Maria Stengler. We know from several parallel recipes that the flour she omits was an important ingredient. Other recipes also add grated cheese, cream, sugar, rosewater, or spices. A waffle batter of white flour, made with plenty of eggs and milk, was luxury enough for most people, though.

To make waffles

Take twelve eggs, beat them, take half a Maß *of sweet milk in the bowl, unsalted butter with it, mix it all together, and add a spoonful of yeast. Stir it well, set it atop an oven, let it rise, and then put it in a waffle iron.*

(Stengler, #88)

1½ HOURS

INGREDIENTS

SERVES 4

250 ml / 1 cup milk (or cream)

½ cube fresh yeast (or 1 teaspoon dry yeast)

50 g / 5 tablespoons butter + extra to grease the iron

6 eggs

200-300 g / c. 2 cups all-purpose flour

Dissolve the yeast in the lukewarm milk and leave to develop for 15 minutes. Melt the butter and beat with the eggs and the milk. Stir in the flour until a thick batter results. Cover and leave to rise in a warm place for 30–45 minutes. You may need to adjust the consistency by adding either milk or flour at this point. The batter must flow from the ladle, but only spread slowly.

Heat and grease the waffle iron. Not much fat is needed to keep this rich batter from sticking, especially if it is made with cream. Drop the batter into the iron by the ladleful and bake golden brown. Be careful not to fill the iron completely as the yeast causes the batter to expand.

Almond Tart

This tart, rich, white and sweet, represents the height of indulgence. It can be prepared from non-seasonal ingredients and could, in theory, be whipped up in a camp kitchen if you had enough cash and wanted to impress people. Certainly it was the kind of thing wealthy hosts would serve honoured guests. Numerous variations survive, including some using whole egg or egg yolk and even one with a meringue-like topping on the filling. This is a basic version:

An almond tart
If you want to make an almond tart, take the whites of eggs and a little grated bread. Take almonds, grind them up small and add rose or lavender water. Add these to the eggs, add sugar, and make a bottom crust as for a tart.

(Stengler, #12)

INGREDIENTS

FOR ONE TART

4 egg whites (more if they are small eggs)
250 g / ½ lb ground blanched almonds
250 g / 1¾ cups powdered sugar
2 tablespoons rosewater
2–3 tablespoons breadcrumbs
Pastry crust

75 MINUTES

Beat the egg whites to stiff peaks. Carefully fold in the powdered sugar and almonds and add the rosewater. Cover the bottom of a pie shell with a thin layer of breadcrumbs, spread the almond mixture on top and bake at 180°C / 350°F for 45–50 minutes or until a toothpick inserted in the centre comes out clean. Cover the top if it browns too much.

If desired, almond tarts can be covered with a meringue topping of beaten egg white and sugar or a thin layer of decoratively cut marzipan. They are also very attractive baked as portion-sized tartlets.

Roast Apples

Stuffed roast apples play a central role in a popular Eulenspiegel tale and were popular as a small treat. Most surviving recipes are highly complex, often involving the fruit being battered and deep-fried. In the story Till Eulenspiegel simply roasts his apples by the fire, just as a Landsknecht surely would. Balthasar Staindl also records a comparatively simple recipe:

Take good apples, not too large, that are not very sour. Do not peel them. Cut off a slice first, then hollow out the apples individually so that an outside layer remains standing. Take an honest amount of almonds, pound them, and add them to chopped apples, then add raisins, cinnamon powder, sugar, and break a fresh egg into it. Fill this into the apples and put the slices back onto them. Make little skewers and stick them in so that the slices stay on the filling. Then take fat into a broad baking dish, let it heat up, cover it with a lid with embers on top, that way it turns nicely brown. [...] Serve it last, this is a good dish.

(Staindl, #43)

1 HOUR

INGREDIENTS

DESSERT FOR 4

- 4 large aromatic apples
- 1 egg
- 100 g / 4 oz raisins
- 50 g / 2 oz ground almonds
- Sugar
- Cinnamon
- Butter

Carefully cut a 2 cm thick slice off the top of each apple and reserve. Hollow out the fruit carefully. Discard the cores and chop the rest of the fruit you removed, then mix it with the egg, raisins, and almonds. Season to taste with sugar and cinnamon. Fill the hollowed-out apples, cover them with the slices and secure with toothpicks. Arrange the apples in a buttered baking dish and cook in a 200°C / 400°F oven for 30 minutes. Serve hot.

Simple Landsknechts would hardly have used sugar and almonds to fill their apples, but the principle must have been similar. That roast apples were filled is the point on which the joke of the Eulenspiegel story hinges.

May Dish

This is a seasonal treat described in the Swiss *Libellus de lacte*, a mid-sixteenth century learned treatise on dairy products. A similar dish is also mentioned in Anna Wecker's 1598 cookbook, though hers is more buttery and firmer. As spring brought new plant growth and milk became plentiful, dairy products were relished by all. May butter—unsalted and unboiled—was a universal pleasure, as were rich, buttery egg dishes. This May Dish, by contrast, is the kind of refined delicacy a wealthy host might serve an officer. It makes a decorative dessert course and is very refreshing chilled.

Cibus Maiis

Melca *or freshly curdled milk is also seasoned with sugar together with butter, a dish that is served at feasts crowned with flowers stuck into it. It is called May food, since it is mostly eaten at this time, when much springtime sweetness from the feed passes into milk and butter.*

(Libellus de lacte, p. 38)

20 MINUTES

INGREDIENTS

DESSERT FOR 4

100 g / ½ cup butter

500 g / 2 cups quark or cottage cheese

100-150 g / ½-¾ cup sugar

Edible flowers

Melt the butter on a low heat, but take care not to boil it. Beat the quark or cottage cheese with the sugar in a bowl and slowly add the liquid butter, stirring constantly. Keep stirring as the mixture cools and sets, then refrigerate. Serve cold, freshly decorated with edible flowers.

Daisies, buttercups, the yellow flowers of dandelions, and violets are all safely edible as long as they have not been treated with pesticides. Taken from a garden or meadow nearby, they add colour and a pleasant scent to the meal. If you are not sure, err on the side of caution—most commercially sold flowers are heavily sprayed and not suitable for eating.

A NIGHT DRINK

A Night Drink

Communal drinking, especially among men, was common at all levels of society, and several sources record that salty and highly seasoned foods were served to stimulate thirst on such occasions. Few concrete recipes survive, but Hieronymus Bock records the description of one such drinking bout that began with dinner and could continue until late at night. The scene plays out in a wealthy home, but the foods he describes are not notably luxurious. There is no reason to think that Landsknechts would have been averse to such celebrations, though they were not daily occasions.

... and though all manner of food and drink of meat and fish were served, several are not content with this and start to cook themselves. One would have bacon soup, another a soup of sour milk, the third wants fried eggs. Some eat raw kippers, raw bratwurst sausage, or have herring from the butt served up raw with vinegar and onions, or at least eat the sauerkraut from cabbage butt for a nightcap. Often the cook has to fry white bread in butter, the drinkers call that thrushes or in Latin scala vini, *a good wine ladder.*

(*Teutsche Speißkammer*, p. CXVI)

Modern observers easily interpret this as a kind of cocktail canapés, small, intensely flavoured nibbles to be served with drinks. That is certainly not an implausible reading and if you are planning a drinking party, you could do worse than to go by that. Raw sauerkraut may not be for everyone, but it has its appeal. Eating raw bratwurst is not recommended, but sausage meat made freshly by a butcher can be perfectly safe. You can serve fried eggs (see p. 52) as nibbles the way we would hard-boiled ones, and kippers or an early form of deli herring work equally well.

SALT HERRING WITH ONIONS

INGREDIENTS

SERVES 4

4 salt herrings

1 onion

4 tablespoons vinegar

10 MINUTES PREPARATION, 1 HOUR STEEPING

Wash the herrings thoroughly, remove heads and fins (if any), and bone them. They can be served whole or in bite-sized pieces. Finely dice the onion, arrange the fish in a deep serving plate, strew with the onions, and drizzle with the vinegar. Let rest for an hour before serving.

SCALA VINI

INGREDIENTS

SERVES 4

4 slices white bread

50 g / 5 tablespoons butter

10 MINUTES

Cut the bread into palm-sized pieces. Melt half the butter in a pan and brown half the bread slices in it. The bread soaks up the butter quickly, so be sure to move the pieces around to prevent them from sticking and burning. Prepare the other half the same way. Serve warm.

Further Reading

INTRODUCTORY WORKS

Though Landsknechts are famous in popular culture, there is still very little published about them in English. A reasonable introduction is the illustrated Landsknecht Soldier volume in Osprey's Warrior series (Richards, John: Landsknecht Soldier 1486–1560, Oxford 2002), but most literature on the topic is in German.

Much the same is true for the history of German cuisine, an underappreciated topic in international culinary history. An excellent overall introduction is found in *Beyond Bratwurst*, the second volume in Reaktion Book's Food and Nations series (Heinzelmann, Ursula: *Beyond Bratwurst. A History of Food in Germany*, London 2014). The sixteenth century specifically is covered in an academic study that is found only in research libraries (Bach, Volker: *The Kitchen, Food and Cooking in Reformation Germany*, Lanham 2016).

SOURCES

Many of the sources used in this book are available freely online, making research far easier than it used to be. This list only includes some of the most important or interesting ones.

The earliest printed cookbook in German was the *Kuchenmaistrey*, first published in Nuremberg in 1486 and reprinted regularly for over a century. Its 220 recipes describe the cuisine of a wealthy patrician household. The second edition of 1490 is on the internet ***(http://diglib.hab.de/inkunabeln/276-quod-2/start.htm)***.

Another influential and interesting recipe collection was first published in 1544 in Augsburg. Balthasar Staindl's *Ein sehr künstlichs und nutzlichs Kochbuch* was reprinted repeatedly well into the seventeenth century. Its style is bourgeois, but like all printed cookbooks of the time, it targets a wealthy readership. The edition of 1569 is on the internet ***(https://reader.digitale-sammlungen.de/de/fs1/object/display/bsb10990136_00005.html)***.

A manuscript that belonged to Sabina Welser of the patrician Welser family of Augsburg also dates to the middle of the sixteenth century. It is organised in a broadly thematic fashion, often including several versions of a dish. A modern edition was published as a book (Stopp, Hugo [Hg.]: *Das Kochbuch der Sabina Welserin*. Heidelberg, 1980). A transcription and English translation are also available online ***(https://www.uni-giessen.de/fbz/fb05/germanistik/absprache/sprachverwendung/gloning/tx/sawe.htm) (http://www.daviddfriedman.com/Medieval/Cookbooks/Sabrina_Welserin.html)***.

Two more very interesting manuscripts were lost in the World Wars and only exist in more or less reliable print editions from the nineteenth century. One is the recipe book of Maria Stengler, another Augsburg patrician, dated 1554. (Anon.: *Augspurger Kochbuoch darinnen enthalten fürtreffliche Rezepte für Frawen und Junckfrawen*. Augsburg, 1886; online ***https://www.uni-giessen.de/fbz/fb05/germanistik/absprache/sprachverwendung/gloning/tx/stenglerin-kochbuch-1554.pdf/view***).

The provenance of the so-called *Klosterkochbuch* is even less clear. It seems to originate with the former Dominican monastery in Leipzig, but only survives in a heavily modernised print edition of 1856 (Otto, Bernhard [Hg.]: *Dreihundertjähriges deutsches Kloster-Kochbuch*. Leipzig, 1856). Modern reprints were produced in quantity and are readily available in second-hand bookstores.

In 1550, a patriotic defence of German cuisine by the noted physician and botanist Hieronymus Bock was printed in Strasbourg. The *Teutsche Speißkammer* does not include recipes as such, but its detailed descriptions of everyday foods and dining habits make it a valuable source. This text, too, is available online ***(https://reader.digitale-sammlungen.de/de/fs1/object/display/bsb10981330_00001.html)***.

The splendour of Germany's cosmopolitan court cuisine at the end of the sixteenth centuy is reflected in Marx (not Max) Rumpolt's *New Kochbuch* of 1581. The author was a culinary star of his day, personal cook to the archbishop-elector of Mainz, and his recipes combine worldly experience and precise observation with a sometimes striking degree of arrogance. A modern reprint was produced in 1977 (Rumpolt, Marx: New Kochbuch. Frankfurt [Main], 1977), but the text is also available online ***(http://diglib.hab.de/wdb.php?dir=drucke/2-3-oec-2f)***.

A similar feat is attempted by Franz de Rontzier's *Kunstbuch von mancherley Essen*. The cook to the Duke of Brunswick and Lüneburg published his book in 1598. It is especially interesting for brief lists of variations on almost every dish. Unfortunately, this work is not yet available online. A modern reprint can sometimes be found in libraries (de Rontzier, Frantz: *Kunstbuch von mancherley Essen*. München, 1979).

Anna Wecker's *Köstlich new Kochbuch* of 1597 gives us a view of the wealthy bourgeois cuisine of the time. This work, dealing mainly with invalid cookery, was reprinted repeatedly and is especially interesting for its precise descriptions of cooking techniques. A modern commented reprint exists (Wecker, Anna: *Ein köstlich new Kochbuch von allerhand Speisen*. Munich, 1977), but the text is also available online ***(https://daten.digitale-sammlungen.de/~db/0002/bsb00028737/images/)***. Both are of the Amberg edition of 1598.

Though they are harder to read, earlier manuscript recipe collections can be very useful for reconstructing Landsknecht cooking. Popular cuisine was often conservative. One important example is the recipe collection ascribed to Meister Hans, a manuscript that mixes complex and simple dishes. A modern edition exists (Ehlert, Trude: *Maister Hannsen des von Wirtenberg koch*. Frankfurt [Main], 1996) and the text is now available online through the CoReMa project ***(http://gams.uni-graz.at/o:corema.bs1#Bs1_017r)***.

Three manuscripts from Austria that belong to a related tradition were transcribed and published together in book form. Especially the Innsbruck manuscript is interesting since it includes many more humble dishes (Aichholzer, Doris: *„Wildu machen ain guet essen ..." Drei mittelhochdeutsche Kochbücher: Erstedition, Übersetzung, Kommentar*. Berne, 1999).

Two further interesting, but short recipe collections are found online. One is, probably spuriously, ascribed to Meister Eberhard, cook to Duke Henry of Landshut. It contains several recipes that remained popular over a century later ***(https://www.uni-giessen.de/fbz/fb05/germanistik/absprache/sprachverwendung/gloning/tx/feyl.htm)***. Another recipe collection from the beginning of the sixteenth century comes from the Inn valley in Bavaria and includes several interesting dairy recipes ***(https://www.uni-giessen.de/fbz/fb05/germanistik/absprache/sprachverwendung/gloning/tx/kb-dann.htm)***.